Styling
Made Simple

Styling Made Simple

KATY HOLDER

hardie grant publishing

CONTENTS

CELEBRATIONS   63

STYLING MADE SIMPLE

INTRODUCTION

The idea for this book came about while I was styling my last cookbook, *A Moveable Feast*, which was all about food you cook then take somewhere, such as a picnic by a river, lunch at a friend's house or afternoon tea in the garden. While photographing that book, I added lots of styling elements to show how nature and other everyday objects can be easily incorporated into styling ideas to use at home, in the garden and when celebrating.

I have been a food stylist for more than 20 years, but on endless occasions I have been asked to style tables and other bits and pieces as well. I also love styling my own home and garden using bits and bobs I find around the place. I've moved countries a few times, yet in every move several very large stones collected on a beach many years ago are packed and unpacked to feature in some sort of display in my new home.

This book, which is a collection of some of my favourite simple styling ideas, is divided into two sections. The first is a collection of projects showing how to style with everyday objects like luggage tags, glass jars, driftwood and noodle boxes; the second half shows fun ways to style your celebrations, such as Christmas, weddings, birthday parties, Halloween and Easter.

What all the projects have in common is that they are simple but effective, and making them can give you a real sense of satisfaction and achievement. Sure you could go out and buy your gift tags for Christmas, but if you can find a spare hour or two, why not create your own personalised tags and make your gifts that much more special? And take the humble

NOTE
Please be aware that in some circumstances it is illegal to take things from nature, such as rocks and wood. I encourage you to acquire the materials used in projects in this book from sustainable and legal sources only.

jam jar: instead of putting it into the recycling bin next time you've finished with it, you could turn it into a pretty hanging jar or upcycle it with a lick of chalkboard paint.

Many of the ideas in this book are for styling around your own home, but lots of them make great gifts too, such as the pompom branch mobile (*see* p. 20) or the pompom branches (*see* p. 17) – otherwise known in our house as Dr Seuss' Truffula Tree!

Special celebrations provide the perfect time to have fun with styling. Planning and organising these events – weddings, parties, Christmas etc – can be as much (if not more!) fun as the actual day of the celebration, and putting your personal touch on an event you're hosting can be extremely satisfying, especially when your guests appreciate your efforts.

With the book's name *Styling Made Simple* as my guide, I kept simplicity in mind while creating the projects – if it all got too complicated, a project simply didn't make the cut. There are one or two slightly more challenging projects, but nothing that requires special tools or equipment. The most exotic it gets is a hot-glue gun, which, I must say, is well worth acquiring if you don't yet have one – they are so much fun to use and surprisingly cheap.

My main aim with this book is to inspire you to create, whether you follow my ideas exactly or just take them and run with them. In the words of my sister Emma, 'It isn't rocket science'; sometimes all that is needed to give you the impetus to start is just being shown how simple something is. Even if you don't think of yourself as being creative, let me assure you that deep down inside everyone there's a creative person just waiting to be let out. I hope this book will help set that person in you free!

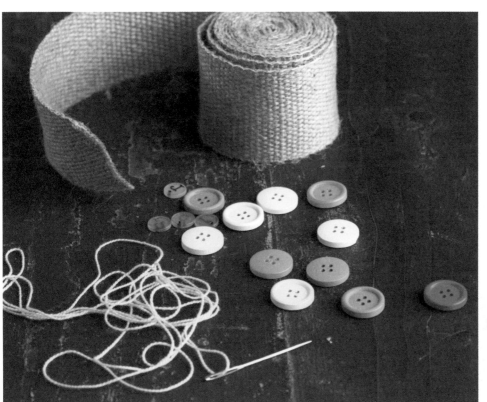

PROJECTS

STYLING WITH JARS

Whenever I finish a jar of jam, marmalade or olives, I always think it's a shame to put the jar in the recycling bin without reusing it. So I started collecting different types of jars and this got me thinking about all the things I could do with them. Occasionally I go a step further, like the time I bought six jars of jam and decanted the jam into plastic tubs, just so I could use the pretty jars for a project I had in mind!

RUSTIC-CHARM JARS

Make these for a rustic wedding, an afternoon tea in the garden or a sunset picnic by a river.

WHAT TO DO

1. Wrap a selection of jars in strips of hessian and/or other fabric of your choice. It's up to you how wide you make the material; it could be so wide that it almost covers the entire jar, or narrower so you can still see through the jar.

2. Secure the material by tying it with rustic string or coloured twine (depending on your colour scheme). If using hessian, you could also tie a thinner strip of hessian around the jar to keep the wider piece in place.

3. Add a little water and fill each jar with flowers of your choice – use whatever takes your fancy at the florist and/or best suits your theme.

YOU WILL NEED:

▼ old jars in different shapes and sizes

▼ hessian and/or fabric of your choice

▼ rustic string or coloured twine

▼ fresh flowers of your choice

CANDLE-LIT JARS

Wide-rimmed jars are best for these pretty decorations.

WHAT TO DO

1. Find some interesting foliage that isn't solid, such as fern, bracken or cypress.

2. Curl the foliage around the inside of the jars and then place a few LED tea lights inside. It's not a good idea to use real candles as the foliage could catch fire.

YOU WILL NEED:

▼ **wide-rimmed jars**

▼ **foliage**

▼ **LED tea lights**

JARS OF FIREFLIES

These jars look pretty lined up in long rows on a table or as furniture decorations (either indoors or outdoors). You could even hang them in the trees.

YOU WILL NEED:

battery-operated strings of LED lights, preferably strings with 10–20 lights each (use 1 string of lights per jar; these are available from party shops, Ikea, Christmas shops etc)

white crepe or tissue paper

jars with lids

silver stars

WHAT TO DO

1. On the LED light string, wind the length of wire that doesn't have any lights on it (i.e. the wire closest to the battery pack) around the battery pack to keep things neat and tidy, and then wrap this in white crepe or tissue paper to disguise it. Repeat for however many jars you are making.

2. Put the battery packs into the jars, ensuring you can still see the on/off switches. Leave the lengths of lights outside the jars.

3. Pour in lots of silver stars to cover the battery packs.

4. Once you are ready to use the jars, turn the battery packs on, put the lights in and screw the lids on.

BANANA LEAF-WRAPPED HANGING JARS

If you're entertaining outside, these are a quick way to create atmosphere. Hang them directly from trees or from a line hung between two trees.

1. Tear strips of banana leaves and wrap them around clean jars.

2. To hold the leaves in place, tie rustic string around the middle of the jar.

3. To work out the length of string you'll need to make a hanging loop, wrap another piece of string twice around the jar then make a loop roughly the length you want. Undo and measure the length you have used, adding on 5 cm (2 in) to make tying the knots easier. Make as many lengths as you need.

4. To make the hanging loop, take the measured string and wrap it twice around the top of the jar (in the groove), tying it in a loose single knot once you've gone around twice. Next take the long end of the string over the top of the jar to the opposite side and tuck it under both layers of string – this is why the first knot needs to be loose, otherwise it's too hard to tuck the string under. Pull the string until you have the desired loop length and tie a tight knot. Re-tie the loose knot to make it tight too. Cut off any excess string. Note that if you aren't hanging the jars from hooks, you may want to leave tying the second knot until you have looped the string over the tree branch.

5. Trim the flowers so the flower heads sit just above or at the rim of the jar, otherwise they may interfere with the loop. Fill the jars with enough water to cover the flower stems, add the flowers and hang from trees.

YOU WILL NEED

▼ banana leaves

▼ jars

▼ rustic string

▼ scissors

▼ fresh flowers of your choice

PAINT-DIPPED JARS

Many of us have sample or large pots of paint left over from painting a room or a piece of furniture and this project is an ideal way of using these up.

WHAT TO DO

There are two ways to make these jars, but the preparation is the same for both. Firstly, make handles with the string so the jars can be hung. To do this, take a piece of string about 60 cm (24 in) long and wrap it twice around the top of the jar (in the groove), tying it in a loose single knot once you've gone around twice.

Next take the long end of the string over the top of the jar to the opposite side and tuck it under both layers of string – this is why the first knot needs to be loose, otherwise it's too hard to tuck the string under. Pull the string until you have the desired handle length and tie a tight knot. Re-tie the loose knot to make it tight too.

Next lay some newspaper under your washing line or a clothes horse, or somewhere else where you can hang the pots to dry.

Method 1

1. If you have large pots of paint, simply dip your jars into the paint to the depth you desire, allowing the excess paint to drip off.

2. Using the pegs, hang the jars on your washing line or clothes horse to dry completely, remembering to put some newspaper underneath to catch all the drips.

3. Once dry, you can double dip to give a striped effect, if desired. Choose a contrasting paint colour and dip the jar again, but make it a more shallow dip than the initial one so you can still see the first layer. Leave to dry as before.

Method 2

1. Place a strip of masking tape around each jar at the level you want the paint to go to.

2. Use a paintbrush to apply the colour.

3. Hang to dry.

Note: You might also like to embellish your jars further, adding dots of paint in a contrasting colour, for example.

CHALKBOARD JARS

The uses for these jars are endless – think spices, lollies, buttons, or even as a moneybox. Write the contents of each jar on the band with chalk, as appropriate. You can use either chalkboard paint or chalkboard tape, which is available from many DIY stores.

WHAT TO DO

Method 1

1. Measure how thick you want your band to be (about 5 cm/2 in is a useful size).
2. Carefully stick two pieces of masking tape around the jar, leaving the desired gap in the middle.
3. Paint the gap with two coats of chalkboard paint, leaving to dry completely in between coats.
4. Write the contents of the jar in the band using chalk.

Method 2

1. Simply cut the chalkboard masking tape to the length you need and wrap it around the middle of the jars in a band.
2. If you'd like to also label the lids – especially useful for spice jars – cut circles of tape out and stick these to the lids.
3. Write the contents of the jar in the band (and on the lid, if relevant) using chalk.

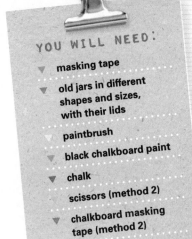

YOU WILL NEED:
- ▼ masking tape
- ▼ old jars in different shapes and sizes, with their lids
- paintbrush
- ▼ black chalkboard paint
- ▼ chalk
- scissors (method 2)
- ▼ chalkboard masking tape (method 2)

STYLING WITH WOOD AND TWIGS

When I go for a walk in a forest or on a wild beach, I keep my eyes peeled to see if I can spot a beautiful weathered piece of wood. A branch can look gorgeous completely unadorned and placed on a shelf or table as a simple decoration. Alternatively it can be dressed up with wool or paint, or used with other branches and pompoms to make a pretty mobile.

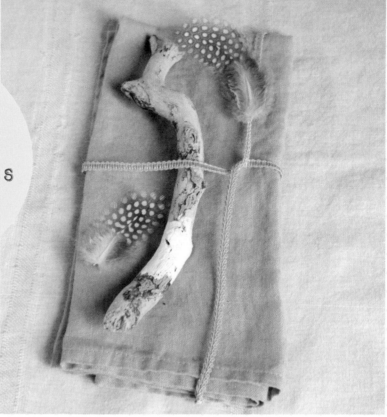

DECORATED TWIG NAPKINS

These painted branches make lovely place settings, or you could always make a single larger one (minus the napkin) to use as a table centrepiece.

YOU WILL NEED:

- paintbrush
- paint in the colour of your choice (to complement the colour of your napkins)
- paint pots (optional)
- weathered twigs and branches, about 10–15 cm (4–6 in) long (the number will depend on how many napkins you are decorating)
- old jam jar or cup
- newspaper
- napkins
- pretty cord or rustic string
- feathers
- luggage tags (optional)

WHAT TO DO

1. Using the paintbrush, paint a band of colour (about 5 cm/2 in wide) around each twig/branch about a quarter of the way up from one end. Allow to dry.

2. Alternatively, put some of the paint in a paint pot (if it isn't already) and dip one end of each twig/branch into the pot, going about one-third to halfway up the length of the twig. Allow any excess paint to drip off, then sit the branch across something like an old jam jar or cup, with newspaper underneath it to catch any paint drips. Allow to dry.

3. Repeat step 1 or 2 (depending on which method you've chosen) two or three times until a solid colour is achieved.

4. Fold the napkins into rectangles and tie about 85 cm (33 in) of pretty cord or rustic string around them in a cross shape (as if you were wrapping a present), but so the cross is off-centre. Tie the cord underneath the napkin so you can't see it.

5. Once your branches are dry, tuck one underneath the cord around each napkin, in the larger space.

6. Pop a feather or two into each napkin for some extra fun. (You could also attach a luggage tag with some string if you like, so you can use the napkins as place settings.)

POMPOM BRANCHES

You could make this for a special dinner or even for Easter, or simply display it as a permanent decorative piece. The pompoms for this project can be bought in discount shops or at art-and-craft shops.

WHAT TO DO

1. Remove any leaves from the branches and ensure the branches are clean and dry.

2. Set up an area, preferably outside or in a very well ventilated space, where you can spray-paint the branches. Spread out several sheets of newspaper (or use a drop sheet if you have one). Lay the branches on the paper and spray them with the white paint, holding the can about 5 cm (2 in) away from the branches. They will probably need two coats of paint. Allow the first coat to dry for about an hour before adding the second coat. Leave to dry completely.

3. Once the branches are dry, glue the pompoms onto them, one at a time. You can either use a blob of craft glue or a hot-glue gun (if you have one; this is not vital). Press each pompom gently onto the branch, trying not to squash them too much. Once the glue is completely dry and the pompoms are firmly stuck on, you can fluff them up a bit if necessary.

4. Gather the branches together and carefully place them into the jar/vase. If the neck of the jar is too wide it will be harder to keep the branches neatly displayed. If your jar isn't see-through and you are having trouble keeping the branches in a neat arrangement, place a large ball of Blu Tack in the bottom of the vase and stick the branches into this to hold them in place.

YOU WILL NEED:

- several long branches or one branch with several branches off it (the length depends on the size of your vase – the branches should preferably be 3 times the length of your vase)
- newspaper
- white spray-paint
- craft glue or hot-glue gun
- small coloured pompoms (diameter of 2.5 cm/1 in is ideal)
- jar or vase with a narrow neck
- Blu Tack (optional)

TWIG MOBILE

You sometimes see these for sale in shops, but they are so simple to make yourself. I use nine twigs for this project, but you can use as many as you like.

WHAT TO DO

1. Arrange the twigs in ascending order of size (or you may wish to mix this up slightly, as I have done).

2. Tie one end of the twine around the middle of the smallest twig, then tie this twig to the middle of the next smallest one, leaving about a 3 cm (1¼ in) gap between the two. Ensure the knots are on the same side so that when you hang the mobile you can't see any knots.

3. Continue in this manner until you've tied all the twigs together.

4. Attach a length of twine to the middle of the top branch to enable the mobile to hang. The length of this twine is up to you, depending on how high or low you want your mobile to hang.

5. Hang the mobile from a hook in the wall or ceiling, then wriggle the twigs around until they're all sitting in nice horizontal lines.

YOU WILL NEED:

▼ 9 weathered twigs of differing lengths

▼ 70–80 cm (28–32 in) length of coloured twine or wool, plus extra for hanging

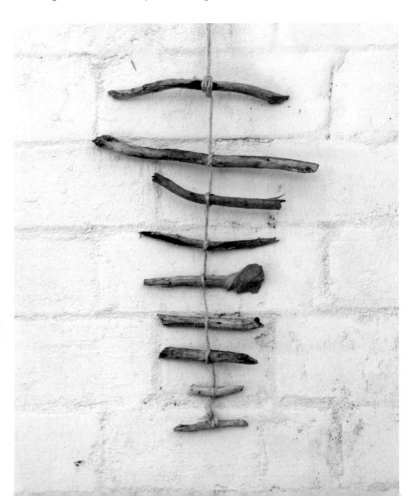

TWIG FRAME

This frame can be used as an ever-changing display, perhaps to highlight your favourite photo of the moment, a drawing from your child or a special postcard.

As this is intended to be a rustic frame, it just sits over the top of photos or postcards, rather than the pictures being held in place by the frame. You simply hang the frame on the wall and then use either a pin or Blu Tack to hold the picture in place.

WHAT TO DO

1. Wrap some wool, string or twine several times around the middle of three of the branches, finishing with a neat knot. Keep the branches separate at this stage.

2. Form the branches into a square with the corners slightly overlapping.

3. Working on one corner at a time and holding the branches at a right angle, take a length of wool about 20 cm (8 in) in length and, leaving about 5 cm (2 in) of one end hanging, start tying the longer length of wool around the branches, working in a sort of 'X' shape. Once the corner feels securely tied, tie the two ends of wool together in a knot at the back of the frame. Repeat for the other three corners, ensuring you tie all the knots at the back.

4. Once you are happy with all the corners, snip off any loose ends of wool.

5. On the branch that doesn't have any wool in the middle, take a length of wool twice the length of how low you want your frame to hang and fold this in half. Bend the loop of wool under the middle of the branch and thread the two ends through, pulling tight. Tie a knot in the wool ends and then your frame is ready to hang.

6. Use either a pin or Blu Tack to secure your picture of choice within the twig frame. You may need to trim your picture to fit the square shape.

YOU WILL NEED:

- coloured wool, rustic string or twine
- 4 weathered branches or twigs of similar lengths (about 25 cm/10 in)
- scissors
- pin or Blu Tack

POMPOM BRANCH MOBILE

My mobile is based on a traditional mobile arrangement. An even simpler version is to make a cross with two branches, secure it in the middle by wrapping wool around both sides of the cross and then hang strands of pompoms off the four ends.

If you can find strings of pompoms already made, use these to save time threading the pompoms. You could also make your own pompoms, like lots of us did as kids. Check out YouTube tutorials on the internet for how to make them.

A word of warning: do not attempt to make this if you are in a hurry. It does take a little time to balance it all up at the end. But do not despair: with a bit of tweaking here and there you will eventually make it work!

YOU WILL NEED:

- cotton thread in the colour of your choice
- needle
- 36 small coloured pompoms (diameter of 2.5 cm/1 in is ideal)
- 4 weathered branches in lengths of about 45 cm (18 in), 25 cm (10 in), 20 cm (8 in) and 15 cm (6 in)
- coloured wool or twine

WHAT TO DO

1. First make three short strands of pompoms. To do this, tie a knot in the end of a piece of cotton thread about 25 cm (10 in) long (this is a bit longer than you need, but it helps to have some excess when tying it to the branch). Using a needle, thread the cotton through the middle of five pompoms, leaving slight gaps (about 5 mm/¼ in) between the pompoms (don't worry about getting this too perfect at this stage – you can tweak this later). Repeat to make the other two short pompom strands.

2. Now make three longer strands. Repeat as above, but use a length of thread about 30 cm (12 in) long and thread seven pompoms onto each strand.

3. Take a moment to mentally label your branches (or you could even put stickers on them that you can remove when you've finished). I find this prevents frustration when tying them all together! Label the longest branch A, then B, C and D (D being the shortest branch).

4. Tie two short strands of pompoms to either end of your shortest piece of wood (D). Tie one long strand to one end of your longest piece of wood (A). Tie another long strand to one end of your next longest branch (B). Tie the remaining pompom strands (one long and one short) to your remaining branch (C), one on either end.

5. Work out how low you want your mobile to hang and cut a length of coloured wool or twine to this length. Tie this to the centre of the longest branch (A).

6 Now comes the assembly of your mobile. Lay the longest branch (A) on a large surface and tie the middle of branch B to the end of A that doesn't have any pompoms on it. Use about 20 cm (8 in) of cotton thread to do this, but make the length between the two branches about 10 cm (4 in), so the excess thread is used to tie the knots. Keep all of the knots a bit loose at this stage (including for steps 7 and 8 following), as you may need to slide them along the branches to balance everything later.

7 Now tie the middle of the shortest branch (D) to the end of B that doesn't have any pompoms on it. Again, use about 20 cm (8 in) of cotton thread to do this, and make the length between the two branches about 10 cm (4 in).

8 Tie the middle of your last branch (C) to the main branch (A), about one-third of the way across from the long pompom strand on A, using about 30 cm (12 in) of cotton thread. The distance between these two branches should be about 20 cm (8 in).

9 Hang the mobile from somewhere like a washing line to get it balanced. Balance it by moving the knots that hold the branches together back and forth along the branches until everything hangs correctly. This is also a good time to tweak the pompoms on their threads, making sure they're all about 5 mm (¼ in) apart.

10 Once everything's balanced and hanging nicely, hang the mobile from a hook in the ceiling.

WEATHERED BRANCH CENTREPIECE

Sometimes the simple things in life really are the best. To me a beautiful twisted and weathered piece of wood is all that is needed as my dinner-table centrepiece. Next time you're out walking in a forest, by a river or on the beach, keep an eye out for weathered pieces of wood, as you never know when they might come in handy. It's funny how some beaches are littered with beautiful pieces of driftwood, while others have nary a twig in sight – it's often just a matter of being in the right place at the right time.

STYLING WITH STONES

I've always loved stones. Whether I'm walking along a river or down at the beach, I can usually be found head down scanning the ground for interesting pebbles and stones instead of watching where I am going! I used them at my wedding as the place settings (the guests took them home to use as decorations or paperweights) and they were also part of the flower arrangements. They liberally decorate my house and garden too.

SILHOUETTE STONES

These stones are great to use as paperweights or simple decorations, or to give as small thank-you gifts. I find there is something very calming about painting the silhouettes on them. If you're not very artistic, look on the internet for silhouette ideas and use these for inspiration and guidance. Some of the most effective shapes are birds on a wire, cats, rabbits and dragonflies.

WHAT TO DO

1. Ensure your stones are clean and dry.
2. Decide what silhouette you are going to draw, using the examples in the photo as a guide if you like.
3. Do a practise sketch on the stone with the pencil, using the eraser if necessary. If you don't feel confident doing this freehand, draw the silhouette onto a piece of paper, cut it out and then draw lightly around the cut-out shape onto the stone.
4. Once you are happy with your sketch, go over the outline with a black texta, then fill in the inside of the image to create the silhouette. If you are right-handed, work from left to right so you don't smudge the drawing. Left-handers should work the other way.

YOU WILL NEED:

▼ stones of different sizes in lighter shades

▼ pencil

▼ eraser

▼ piece of paper (optional)

▼ scissors (optional)

▼ black texta (marker pen)

NAPKIN WEIGHTS

Here's a way to solve the problem of your napkins flying away on your next picnic or outdoor meal! Simply wrap coloured twine around a beautiful stone and put the stone on top of your napkin pile to hold it down in the wind. (Obviously, the stone needs to be big enough to act as a suitable weight.)

You can keep this simple by just tying the twine around an unpainted stone, or embellish the stone with one of the ideas in this chapter and then tie the twine.

IDEAS FOR HOW TO TIE THE TWINE:

▼ Create a cross shape. Do this by working out which way up your stone is going to sit, then wrap a length of twine once around the stone and tie it in a knot at the back, leaving one end long. Holding your finger on the knot, turn the stone 90 degrees and bring the twine up and over the stone to create the cross shape. Tie at the back again. (You can wrap the string around several times before tying, if you prefer.) If your cross is a bit loose, you can always add a small piece of sticky tape on the back.

▼ Make a crazy pattern. Take a length of twine and, leaving about 4 cm (1½ in) hanging out the back to make a knot, start wrapping the twine around and around the stone in different directions until you have a look you like. End with the twine at the back and tie a knot. Cut off any remaining twine.

▼ Make a simple pattern. Take a length of twine and tape down one end on the back of the stone, leaving about 4 cm (1½ in) hanging out to make a knot. Wrap the twine three or four times around one end of the stone only. End with the twine at the back and tie a knot. Cut off any remaining twine.

PAINTED STONES

Although a plain grey or white stone can be a thing of beauty in itself, it is also fun to decorate stones and use them as paperweights, or simply as something lovely to have on your table.

WHAT TO DO

1 Ensure your stones are clean and dry, then try one of the ideas suggested to the left.

2 Whichever method you choose, once the stones are dry, you can write a name on each one in black texta and use the stones as place settings, or write inspirational words (e.g. 'Love', 'You Rock!', 'Happy') on each one. Alternatively, just leave them plain.

YOU WILL NEED:

▼ stones of different sizes

▼ black texta (marker pen; optional)

▼ small paintbrushes

▼ paint in the colour(s) of your choice

▼ masking tape (optional)

DOT PAINTINGS

There's something very therapeutic about dipping the eraser end of a pencil in paint then creating a pattern on a stone. If you're putting more than one colour on your stone, it is easier to have a separate pencil eraser for each colour than it is to wash the eraser in between colours.

If you have a stone that isn't round, you might want to paint a different shape, such as a cross.

WHAT TO DO

1. Ensure your stones are clean and dry.
2. If you are using tubes of paint, squeeze a small amount into a pot or even just onto a piece of newspaper; repeat with all the colours you'll be using.
3. Dip the pencil eraser into the first paint colour, then, starting in the centre of the stone, work your way outwards, adding dots as you go. Work slowly so as not to smudge the dots.
4. Change paint colour and pencil eraser as desired.
5. Allow the paint to dry completely before handling.

YOU WILL NEED:

- stones of different sizes
- paint in the colour(s) of your choice
- small pots for the paint (unless it is already in pots; optional)
- newspaper (optional)
- pencil with an eraser on the end (or several if using different colours)

STACKS OF STONES

I find looking at stacks of pebbles or stones can be quite meditative. The stones you use can be big or small, but ensure they are quite stable otherwise you'll be forever picking them up and restacking them. Place them inside and out, but beware that small children find them irresistible, so you may find yourself rebuilding the stacks on a regular basis if you have kids around! Mind you, that's not necessarily a bad thing, as stacking them can, in itself, be quite meditative too. Better yet, get the kids involved and develop their fine motor skills!

Finding the perfect stones for stacking often involves pure luck – in particular, keep your eyes peeled when you're at the beach or walking along a river. If you don't want to wait for the right stackable stones or pebbles to come along, look for them at garden centres and landscaping suppliers. They're also sometimes available in gift shops, and you can look online for them too.

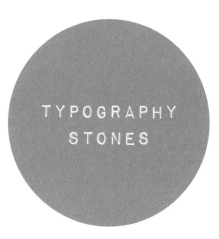

TYPOGRAPHY STONES

This is a simple way to add character to stones, and they can be used in many ways, e.g. as name place settings at a meal or simply as a home decoration. You can often find sheets of typography stickers in craft or discount shops. I particularly like the ones that look like Scrabble letters. If you can't find stickers, you can also paint or write the letters on the stones.

WHAT TO DO

1. Ensure your stones are clean and dry.
2. Think about what you want to spell out on each stone, e.g. you can use just one letter, write a whole name or spell an inspirational word like 'Love'.
3. Stick the letters onto the middle of the stones – it's as simple as that!
4. Alternatively, if you can't find stickers, you can simply paint or write letters or words onto the stones with black paint or texta (you'll need to use stones that are lighter in colour for this to work). It's a good idea to practise painting/writing your message on a piece of scrap paper before working on the stones. If using paint, allow time for it to dry completely.

YOU WILL NEED:

- stones of different sizes
- typography stickers
- black paint and paintbrush (optional)
- black texta (marker pen; optional)
- scrap paper (optional)

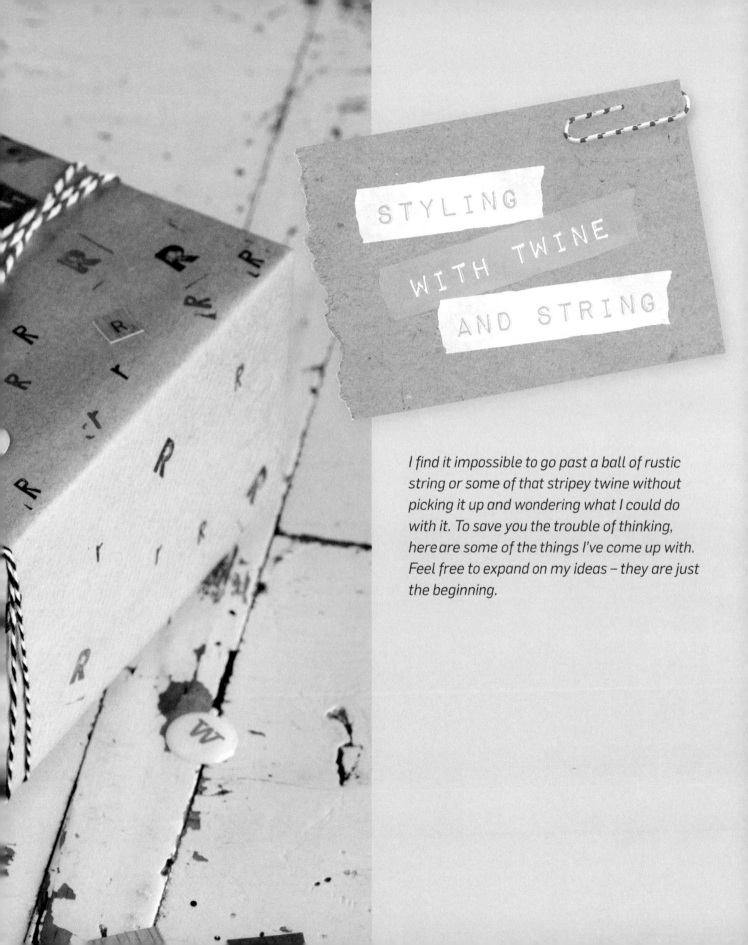

STYLING WITH TWINE AND STRING

I find it impossible to go past a ball of rustic string or some of that stripey twine without picking it up and wondering what I could do with it. To save you the trouble of thinking, here are some of the things I've come up with. Feel free to expand on my ideas – they are just the beginning.

DECORATIVE BALLS OF TWINE

This is a super simple way to store your twine collection and at the same time create a colourful display piece.

WHAT TO DO

1. Depending on the size of the twine balls, either just pop them into the jar in an attractive way or, if they are too large or are in bundles not balls, roll them into balls that will fit into the jar.

2. For added texture and interest, you could also put in balls of different materials, including ceramic and glass.

YOU WILL NEED:

- different coloured and textured balls or bundles of twine
- glass jar with a wide neck
- ceramic, glass or other decorative balls (optional)

ENAMEL-AND-TWINE PLANTERS

Look for old enamel cups and bowls at charity shops and transform them into lovely plant pots. Ensure they have a lip at the top, around which you tie the twine. Succulents are ideal for this project, as they are slow growing so they won't outgrow the container too quickly.

WHAT TO DO

1. Start by putting a 1 cm (½ in) layer of gravel or tiny pebbles in the bottom of the cup or bowl. It is then best to add a 1 cm (½ in) layer of crushed charcoal on top, but this is not vital.

2. Half fill your cup or bowl with soil suitable for your chosen succulent(s) and add one or two plants. Don't overfill the container, as, although slow growing, the succulents will eventually outgrow the container, especially if you are using cups.

3. Add a bit more soil, pressing it down quite firmly and leaving at least a 1 cm (½ in) gap at the top. Add enough water to moisten the soil, but don't flood it.

4. If using white pebbles, put them on top of the soil.

5. To create the loop for hanging, take a long length of twine or string (the length will depend on how low you want your plant to hang) and wrap it twice around the top of the cup/bowl (under the lip), tying it in a loose single knot at the start. Take the longer end of the string over the top of the container so it is opposite the first knot and tuck it under both layers of string, pulling until you have the desired loop length. Tie the string in a tight knot to secure. Re-tie the loose knot so it is also tight. Cut off any excess string.

6. Hang the planter indoors or out; somewhere that gets indirect sunlight is ideal. Water only occasionally, being careful not to over-water.

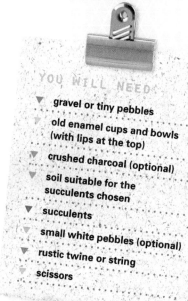

YOU WILL NEED

▼ gravel or tiny pebbles

▼ old enamel cups and bowls (with lips at the top)

▼ crushed charcoal (optional)

▼ soil suitable for the succulents chosen

▼ succulents

▼ small white pebbles (optional)

▼ rustic twine or string

▼ scissors

BUTTON-AND-TWINE 'RIBBONS'

Here's a use for all those spare buttons you have lying around (or am I the only person who has multitudes of them? No, I didn't think so!). You may as well make a few of these at a time, so you have them ready to go next time you want to decorate a gift.

Use buttons with holes that aren't too tiny, otherwise you won't be able to thread the twine through.

YOU WILL NEED:

▼ old buttons

▽ twine or string

▼ needle (optional)

▽ gift tag, if using

WHAT TO DO

1. Think about how you'd like to arrange your buttons before you start threading them. Do you want all the buttons to be the same size or will you have them getting smaller and smaller? Do you want the colour of the buttons to match your wrapping paper or contrast with it? Similarly, do you want to use buttons of a similar hue, or different coloured ones? You can use as many buttons as you like, although I usually go with about six.

2. Thread a long length of twine through the buttonholes. You will probably need to do this without a needle, as most twines are too thick for a needle. If you find a needle with a wide enough eye, it will probably then be too thick to go through the buttonhole! However, if you do find the perfect combination, by all means use a needle, as it will save time. Space the buttons about 5 mm (¼ in) apart. Don't worry too much about this at this stage though, as you can always move them a little once they're threaded, if necessary.

3. Once you have threaded the buttons, use the twine to decorate wrapped gifts. (I find this works best if a fairly plain wrapping paper is used, so that the button-and-twine 'ribbons' really shine.) Simply wrapping the twine once around a gift – either lengthways or across the parcel – and tying it in a knot at the back looks very effective. Alternatively, wrap the twine around the parcel a second time and tie in a bow on top.

4. Attach a gift tag, if required, using matching twine.

CRAZY WRAPPING WITH TWINE

Yes, you could wrap a gift in plain old paper and hand it over, or you could go crazy and really individualise your present. Personally I'd go for the second option every time, and here's how to do it.

If you don't have letter stickers or letter stamps and an ink pad, or don't have the time to get them, find letters in different colours, sizes and fonts on your computer, collate them into a Word document, print them out, cut them out and then stick them onto the paper with glue.

WHAT TO DO

1. Cut the wrapping paper to the right size for your gift.
2. Using the letter stickers and/or stamps and ink pad and/or pens, stick, stamp and/or write the recipient's first initial all over the paper. Lots of different sizes work well.
3. Using the decorated paper and sticky tape, wrap your gift.
4. Next tie loads of twine around the gift. Start by wrapping the twine four or so times around the length of the gift on different angles, then tie in a knot at the back. Next wrap the twine around the top of the gift (about a third of the way down) three or so times, also on different angles and tying at the back. You can use the same coloured twine for this or two different colours, if preferred. Trim off any loose bits of twine.
5. If desired, you can decorate your gift further by adding random bits of washi tape, perhaps wrapping a strip over one corner of the gift.
6. Add a gift tag to your present, if using.

YOU WILL NEED:

- ▼ scissors
- ▼ brown or white wrapping paper
- ▼ sheets of letter stickers and/or letter stamps and ink pad
- ▼ pens in the colour(s) of your choice
- ▼ sticky tape (Scotch tape)
- ▼ twine or rustic string (different colours/ types, if desired)
- ▼ washi tape (optional)
- ▼ gift tags, if using

STYLING WITH LUGGAGE TAGS

I can't walk past a packet of luggage tags without picking them up. Maybe they remind me of the past, but I suspect it has more to do with my childhood love of Paddington Bear! Who can forget that gorgeous old luggage tag tied around his neck with 'Please look after this bear' written on it?

There's a multitude of simple things you can create with tags, apart from their obvious use as a gift tag. Try tying them around jars as a label, on napkins as a place name, hanging them as a Christmas decoration or use them for labelling kids' storage boxes.

Your tag will need a hole in. If it doesn't have a hole, punch one using a hole puncher. Stick an adhesive ring over the hole on both sides of the tag to strengthen the hole.

For suggestions of how to thread twine through luggage tag holes and advice on how much twine you will need to use, see the Handy Hints, Materials and Recipes section on page 175.

MESSAGE TAGS FOR FOOD GIFTS

These tags are really good when giving gifts, especially food gifts. It's fun to write playful things on them. Some of my favourite messages are 'Mmm, Looks Yummy', 'How Exciting!', 'Eat Me!', 'Food Glorious Food' and 'Ooooh! Chocolate!'.

WHAT TO DO

1. Part of the fun of this project is coming up with the messages for your gifts. Think of what message you want to write and then check it will fit on your tag. I always practise on some scrap paper first.

2. As every typography set is different, you'll also need to establish how close together you need to place the letters when stamping, so practise this as well.

3. Once you're confident that your messages are going to fit, get busy stamping them onto the luggage tags!

4. When your food parcels are ready to go, cut the cellophane so that it's large enough to enclose your gift with about 10 cm (4 in) excess at the top. Sit your gift in the middle of the cellophane.

5. Cut the twine to the correct length. The amount of twine you'll need to tie up the cellophane will depend on the size of the parcels. As a guide, small parcels like those in the photo need lengths of about 35–40 cm (14–16 in) each.

6. Thread a luggage tag onto the twine. Bring the cellophane up around the sides of the food parcel and then wrap the twine a couple of times around the top of the gift and tie securely. Tie the twine in a bow (*see* the Handy Hints, Materials and Recipes section on p. 174 for how to tie the perfect bow). (Remember to store the food gifts in the fridge if necessary!)

7. Alternatively you can tie the luggage tags around jars.

YOU WILL NEED:

- scrap paper
- pencil
- wooden typography letters and ink pad
- luggage tags
- scissors
- sheets of cellophane
- twine

MAP TAGS

These can be used in numerous situations, but a novel idea is to use them as place settings at a wedding. Use maps that indicate where the bride and groom are going on their honeymoon or even where the wedding destination is.

YOU WILL NEED:

▼ old or colourful map

  pencil

  luggage tags

▼ scissors

▼ craft glue

▼ hole puncher

▼ white or coloured
  adhesive hole
  puncher rings

▼ pen, or wooden
  typography letters
  and ink pad

  coloured twine, if using

WHAT TO DO

1. Turn the map over and, placing a luggage tag on the back of the map, draw around the edge of the luggage tag to create an outline. Repeat for as many tags as you would like to make.

2. Carefully cut out the map outlines and glue one to each tag. Alternatively cut out sections of maps that will fit on the tags.

3. Turn the tag over and, if it already has a hole, use this as a guide to punch a new hole through the map. If there's no hole, punch one in the centre of one end of the tag.

4. Stick an adhesive ring over each hole on both sides of the tag to strengthen the hole.

5. If using as a gift tag, write or stamp your message on the blank side of each tag. If using as name place settings, write or stamp on the map side.

6. If using twine, thread it through each hole.

CRAFT TAGS

YOU WILL NEED:

▼ **old buttons**

▼ **textured stickers**

▼ **luggage tags**

▼ **piece of paper (optional)**

▼ **wooden typography letters and ink pad**

▼ **washi tape (optional)**

▼ **pen (optional)**

▼ **craft glue**

▼ **twine, if using**

Hunt down all those spare buttons you've never needed to use, like the ones that come with new clothes, and repurpose them into these gorgeous handmade tags. Make a few so you've always got a unique gift tag ready to attach to gifts. Just one thing: ensure the buttons have a flat base, otherwise they can't be glued on.

WHAT TO DO

1. Before actually sticking anything to your luggage tags, play around with arranging the buttons and stickers to create your design on the tag, or even on a piece of paper, to ensure you'll have sufficient room for design elements, plus any wording you want to use. If preferred, you can decorate just one side of the tag and use the blank side for your message. Odd numbers of objects often look best in a design, but that isn't a hard-and-fast rule – it's your tag so design as you will!

2. When you're happy with the design, use the typography letters and ink pad (or simply a pen if you don't have these) to stamp the wording onto the luggage tags. It makes sense to do this step first, because if you muck up the lettering – which happens! – you won't have wasted buttons and stickers as well. Also if you're intending to use the blank side for your message, it is easier to write the message while the other side is still flat, rather than bumpy from the added buttons. (Of course, if you're making several of these tags for future use, you can just add your messages as you need them.)

3. Once all the wording is on, glue on the buttons and add the stickers and washi tape, if using.

4. Add twine at the end, if using.

PERSONALISED NAME TAGS

These are some of the simplest tags to make and can be done by kids and adults alike. Make some for each member of the household so everyone knows where to put their stuff. This is a great rainy-day activity and is doubly good because it encourages kids to label their things. If you like order, keep the tags the same, but for more fun use a selection of tags of different sizes and colours.

WHAT TO DO

1. If using typography letters and ink, have a quick practise of writing names on some scrap paper, so as not to waste any luggage tags. As every typography set is different, you'll also want to establish how close together you need to place the letters when stamping, so practise this as well. Then get stamping!

2. If you are using letter stickers, make sure the names you want to write will fit on the tags.

3. If you have an old-fashioned Dymo (or a modern version of the old style), use this to write the names.

4. Feel free to mix things up, using a combination of typography letters, stickers and the Dymo to create the name tags.

5. If you're sticking the tags to the fronts of drawers or storage boxes, you won't need twine. (In this case, use Blu Tack if you want to be able to remove the tags, or double-sided tape if not.) But if using around jars or tins for pencils etc, add twine to the tags.

YOU WILL NEED:

▼ **scrap paper**

▼ **wooden typography letters and ink pad or sheets of letter stickers or an old-fashioned Dymo label maker (if you have one), or a combination of all three**

▼ **luggage tags**

▼ **Blu Tack (optional)**

▼ **double-sided tape (optional)**

▼ **twine, if using**

FABRIC TAGS

If you already do some crafty-type projects, you're bound to have scraps of fabric left over that would be ideal for these tags. If you don't already have fabric scraps, you can pick them up very cheaply in the sale bins at fabric and craft shops.

Because it can be fiddly cutting out small pieces of fabric, I tend to make these so that the whole of one side of the tag is the design and then I write on the other. But you can also simply put one strip of fabric across the bottom of each tag so you'll still have room to add a message as well.

WHAT TO DO

1. First, decide on your design – see below for a few ideas.
2. Only start cutting the fabric once you're fairly certain of your design, although as most of the designs use only small bits of fabric you can usually start again if you muck things up.
3. Glue the fabric to the luggage tags according to your design.
4. Allow to dry before adding any written messages on the blank sides of the tags.
5. You can also use fabric instead of twine to attach the tags. Cut strips of fabric about 20 cm (8 in) long and 1 cm (½ in) wide. Double each piece over lengthwise and thread about 2 cm (¾ in) of the folded end through the luggage tag hole. Thread the two loose ends of the fabric through the loop created by the folded end and pull gently to secure. Don't worry about any frayed edges – these just add to the charm.

YOU WILL NEED:

- scissors
- fabric (scraps are fine)
- craft glue
- luggage tags
- twine, if using
- stickers (optional)

IDEAS FOR DESIGNS:

- See if the fabric can dictate the design. For example, the green fabric on the Christmas tree tag (pictured) instantly said 'Christmas tree' to me when I looked at it.
- If you have a patterned fabric (like the one with orange dots pictured), play on the theme, cutting out larger dots for a fabric with small dots, for example, or squares for a square-patterned fabric. Alternatively, try the opposite – a square pattern for round dots.
- If the gift is for a birthday present, cut out the recipient's initial from some fabric and stick that on, perhaps adding an exclamation mark too. If it's for Mother's Day you could cut out the letters 'Mum' and stick them on, adding a heart sticker as well.
- For Christmas tags, cut either strips of the same fabric or different coloured fabric and create a tag like the stripey Christmas tree one pictured. Add a star sticker to finish it off.

WASHI TAPE TAGS

These tags can be as simple or as elaborate as you want. If you like things to match, use the same washi tape on your tags as the tape used to secure wrapping paper on Christmas and birthday presents. For this to be most effective, use either plain wrapping paper and a more decorative tape or a patterned paper with a single-colour tape.

WHAT TO DO

1. Decide on a design for your tags. I've suggested a few below, but much of the fun is deciding how you want your tags to look. The occasion you are making your tags for (such as Christmas or a wedding) may dictate your design, or you may design the tags around whatever washi tape you have to hand.

2. To keep the tags looking smart, ensure the washi tape edges are neat. Do this by folding the ends of the tape around the edges of the tag, instead of cutting the tape to the exact width of the tag. You can only do this, however, if you're not making double-sided tags (see next step); if you are, you just need to ensure you cut lovely neat ends.

3. If you like, you can design your tags so that they're double-sided, i.e. one side is decorated and the other is blank, so you can write a message on the blank side. However, if you do this remember that you can't have any excess tape from the other side appearing on the blank side.

4. If you make double-sided tags, ensure the decorated side of your tag is showing when you attach it to your parcel. If using twine and none is supplied with the tag, buy twine that matches the colour of your tape.

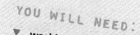

YOU WILL NEED:

- ▼ washi tape of your choice
- ▼ luggage tags
- ▼ twine, if using
- ▼ other decorations, such as feathers (optional)

IDEAS FOR DESIGNS:

- ▼ The most simple design is to put a single piece of washi tape across the bottom of each tag or diagonally across the middle.

- ▼ Alternatively, layer contrasting colours of tape onto the tags.

- ▼ Another very simple but effective design is to tape a single feather to each tag. Use either a feather you have found or you can buy bags of feathers from craft shops.

STYLING WITH NOODLE BOXES

Noodle boxes can be used on a multitude of occasions and can be themed very easily. They're great for serving food at parties and for transporting food to picnics or friends' houses. Alternatively, use them instead of a gift box or to hold jewellery, or simply to store a few precious things.

One of the first times I used them was at my son's second birthday party. Instead of putting all the food out on platters and having the kids eat only the cakes and chips, I made up the same selection of birthday food, but put some of it into noodle boxes instead. Each box had a couple of sandwiches, a small bunch of grapes, some strawberries and some vegetable sticks in it. It was amazing: nearly every kid ate everything in their box and then we moved onto cake and other goodies.

ASIAN BOXES

These boxes are the perfect finishing touch when serving dishes such as noodle salads, fried rice and sushi. For decoration, you can use anything related to Asia such as typography and pictures. You could even use pages from an Asian newspaper, which you can buy from some newsagencies or in your local Chinatown.

WHAT TO DO

1. Each box will be decorated with vertical strips of Asian-themed paper. The length of these decorative strips will depend on what materials you have to hand. If using a newspaper, for example, you can cut one long strip, but if your materials aren't that long you'll need to cut two strips, one for each side of the box.

2. If cutting two strips, cut them long enough to allow a little extra to stick on the bottom of the noodle boxes, rather than ending at the bottom edge (this makes the boxes look neater). To measure the lengths you'll require, open the lids (flaps) of one of the noodle boxes and measure from the slit in the lid on one side of the box, down the side of the box and underneath the box for at least 1 cm (½ in).

3. If making one long strip, work out the length required by opening the lids of one of the noddle boxes and measuring the length from the slit in the lid on one side, down the side, underneath, then back up the other side to where the flap tucks in.

4. Having established if you need one or two strips, you now need to work out the width of the strips. Again this will depend on the size of the noodle boxes. For smaller boxes (9–10 cm/3½–4 in across the top of the box, measuring in the same direction as the wire handles), make the strips about 4 cm (1½ in) wide. For larger boxes (11–12 cm/4½–5 in across the top of the box), make them about 6 cm (2½ in) wide.

5. Cut strips of your chosen decorative paper to the length and width required.

6. Starting at the slit in the box's flap, glue the strip(s) of decorative paper to the noodle box (as described in steps 2 or 3), pressing gently on any air bubbles to get rid of them. Add a strip of washi tape to each top edge, if desired.

7. Stick a pair of chopsticks to each box with a short strip of washi tape.

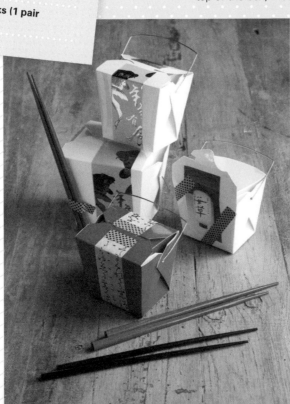

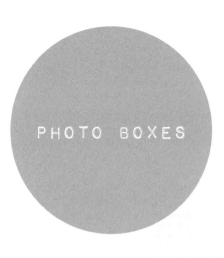

PHOTO BOXES

You can get as silly or as serious as you like with these boxes. If they are for a child's birthday party, you can plaster the boxes with your favourite pics of the child. Or if you're having friends around for dinner, hunt out old photos you might have of them, or even ask your friends to send you some, without telling them why. Printing them out on glossy photo paper gives the best results, but even printing on plain white paper will work.

WHAT TO DO

1. The size your photos need to be will depend on the size of the noodle boxes; ideally you should be able to fit one photo on each flat side of the noodle box. Cut the photos to fit if necessary.

2. Glue one photo onto the two larger sides of each noodle box, i.e. so each box will have two photos on it. Of course, you can stick on more photos than this if you'd like to make a collage.

3. If you like, decorate the boxes further with stickers or cut-outs relevant to the occasion.

4. If you have an old-fashioned Dymo label maker, you could create messages relevant to the occasion using this.

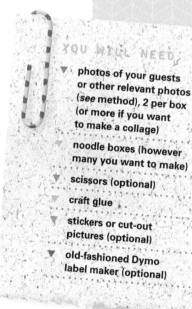

YOU WILL NEED

▼ photos of your guests or other relevant photos (see method), 2 per box (or more if you want to make a collage)

▼ noodle boxes (however many you want to make)

▼ scissors (optional)

▼ craft glue

▼ stickers or cut-out pictures (optional)

▼ old-fashioned Dymo label maker (optional)

ALL
MAPPED OUT

Maps – old or new – hint at journeys past and those still to come. I could (and do) spend hours planning dream trips, some of which will stay as dreams and some of which I know will happen. Start the conversation with these map boxes.

WHAT TO DO

1. There are many ways to do this. This project describes two different ways, although you can create your own design if you'd prefer. The first way covers all four sides of the noodle box. To do it this way, first cut two pieces of map paper the same size. The width of the paper needs to be the width of one side of the noodle box (the 'smooth' side, i.e. the side that doesn't have any joins in it), plus enough to cover half of each side where the joins are. The height of the paper needs to be the height from the bottom of the box up to where the noodle box fastens at the top, plus an extra 1 cm (½ in) for folding under the bottom of the box.

2. Using the craft glue, stick the first piece of map paper to one of the smooth sides, wrapping it around the edges and also folding it underneath the box. Add strips of washi tape at the top where it tucks inside the box. On the sides with joins, at the top edge, tuck the paper inside at the top edges of the box and stick it down with washi tape. Repeat with the other side.

3. Alternatively, you can decorate your box more simply by wrapping one long strip of map all the way around the middle of the box in a vertical direction. Cut the map paper to size. For small noodle boxes (9–10 cm/3½–4 in across the top of the box, measuring in the same direction as the wire handles), you'll need a strip of map about 32 cm (12½ in) long and 3 cm (1 in) wide for each box. For larger boxes (12 cm/5 in across the top of the box), you will need a strip of map about 42 cm (16½ in) long and 5 cm (2 in) wide for each box. Once you've cut the paper, glue it all the way around the box vertically, having some of it go up about 1 cm (½ in) onto the flaps of the box. If you do a horizontal strip instead, you'll need a strip of map that is 3 cm (1¼ in) wide and 1–2 cm (½ in) longer than the circumference of the box.

4. You can leave your boxes like this or embellish them more. For example, if you have any old stamps you could stick one or two onto each box. Alternatively, wrap some rustic brown string three times around the lower part of each box, about a quarter of the way up from the bottom. Tie the string securely and then tuck a small luggage tag into the string.

- tape measure
- scissors
- old map or map wrapping paper
- craft glue
- noodle boxes (however many you want to make)
- travel-themed or a single-colour washi tape
- old stamps (optional)
- brown string (optional)
- small brown luggage tags (optional)

MESSAGE BOXES

These are great for parties that have a theme, such as New Year's Eve or a birthday party. I like to fill the boxes with salads, fried rice or noodle dishes. Ensure your boxes are leak-proof before adding any liquids, such as dressings.

WHAT TO DO

1. Think up fun messages for your boxes relevant to your event, such as 'It's nearly the new year!', 'Let's celebrate' or 'It's time to party!'.

2. If using a printer and printer labels, find a font you like and check that the size of your message will fit onto the labels you're using and across the boxes; it's a good idea to practise this on plain paper first so you don't waste any labels. Once you've practised, print your messages onto the labels and stick them onto the boxes.

3. Alternatively, use letter stickers to form the words, again, checking in advance that they'll all fit, or use the Dymo to print them.

4. Decorate each box with washi tape, as desired. One idea is to create frames with the tape around the edges of the boxes.

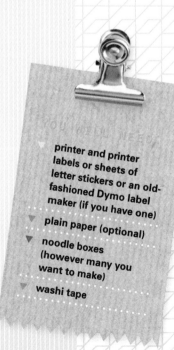

YOU WILL NEED

- printer and printer labels or sheets of letter stickers or an old-fashioned Dymo label maker (if you have one)
- plain paper (optional)
- noodle boxes (however many you want to make)
- washi tape

HESSIAN-AND-TWINE BOXES

I like to use these boxes as gift boxes, but you could also make one to keep jewellery or keepsakes in.

YOU WILL NEED:

▼ scissors

▼ piece of hessian or linen (*see* note p. 51)

▼ noodle boxes (however many you want to make)

▼ wide-eyed needle (to fit twine through)

▼ twine

▼ 4 buttons per box

▼ craft glue

WHAT TO DO

1. Cut strips of hessian/linen to wrap around the boxes (note that the lengths mentioned here allow for a little overlap at the top of each box). For small noodle boxes (9–10 cm/3½–4 in across the top of the box, measuring in the same direction as the wire handles), you'll need a strip of hessian about 34 cm (13½ in) long and 4 cm (1½ in) wide for each box. For larger boxes (12 cm/5 in across the top of the box), you will need a strip of hessian about 42 cm (16½ in) long and 6 cm (2½ in) wide for each box.

2. Thread the needle with a 20 cm (8 in) length of twine. Make a single stitch about 1–2 cm (½–1 in) from the end of the fabric and leave about an 8 cm (3 in) length of twine hanging from the end of the fabric – this is for securing the box later.

3. Sew on three buttons about 3 mm (⅛ in) apart. Once the third button is attached, secure the thread on the underside of the linen and cut off any excess twine.

4. Take another short length of twine and attach the fourth button onto the other end of the fabric so that it will line up with the other three buttons. It should be about 4 cm (1½ in) from the end of the fabric.

5. The next step involves wrapping the hessian around each box, perpendicular to the silver handle on the box. First, turn the hessian over, so that the buttons are sitting underneath. Dab glue onto the base of the box and sit it in the middle of the hessian piece. Before pressing it to stick to the hessian, bring the ends of the hessian up over the box to make sure the buttons are going to be sitting nicely on top of the box. Adjust the position of the box base on the hessian if necessary.

6. Once you're happy with where the buttons are sitting, press the box down gently so that it sticks to the hessian. Next add glue to two sides of the box and stick the hessian to these sides. (Note: You don't stick the hessian to the flaps on top of the box.) Leave to dry.

7. Put your gift into the box, close the box flaps, overlap the edges of the hessian so the buttons all line up and then loop the excess 8 cm (3 in) length of twine around both end buttons a few times (looping in a figure 8 works well) to secure the hessian around the box.

8 For extra decoration wrap another length of twine all the way around the box. To do this, cut a piece of twine twice the length of both sides and the base of the box. Fold the twine in half and hook the loop around the first button in the group of three (i.e. the one closest to the fabric's end) then wrap the twine underneath the box and up the other side, tying it around the single button.

Note: The size of the piece of hessian or linen required will depend on how many boxes you are making and what size the boxes are. Use the measurements provided in step 1.

STYLING WITH WRAPPING PAPER

For me, it's not just about the gift – it's about how I wrap it too. At Christmas I spend far too much time choosing paper, ribbons and tags, and I love admiring my pile of wrapped gifts at the end. Even if you only have one gift to wrap, this chapter has a few simple ideas that will make your gift stand out from the crowd.

One of the easiest shapes to wrap and to show off beautiful wrapping is a box, so it's worth buying a gift box to put your present in. Gift boxes (and plain cardboard ones) can be bought quite cheaply from discount stores and some party shops. You might think it's crazy to gift wrap a gift box, but it means you can personalise it.

CHRISTMAS - STORY WRAPPING

If you don't want to cut up one of your own storybooks, find one in a second-hand shop. Try to ensure the pages you cut out from the book are easily identified as being from a Christmas story. This idea works best on medium- to large-sized gifts.

YOU WILL NEED:

▼ brown paper
▼ sticky tape (Scotch tape)
▼ washi tape (optional)
▼ scissors
▼ red or green card
▼ old Christmas storybook
▼ craft glue
▼ striped twine
▼ luggage tags (optional)

WHAT TO DO

1 First wrap your gift in brown paper, keeping the joins neat and any folds crisp. Use washi tape instead of sticky tape to secure, if desired.

2 Cut out a square of red or green card that's about 15 cm x 15 cm (6 in x 6 in).

3 Next cut out a shape from one of the pages of the Christmas storybook (ensuring the page you choose looks Christmassy). Shapes such as a star, reindeer or Christmas tree work well. The shape should be about 10–12 cm (4–5 in) in height, so that it fits within the square of card you've cut out. (Of course, if you have a much larger parcel, you can make the square and the shape bigger.) Cookie cutters are ideal for this: simply place one on a page, check which words or picture will appear in the shape, draw around the cookie cutter, then cut the shape out.

4 Stick the story shape to the centre of the card square, and then stick this onto the front of your parcel. Sticking it at one end of the parcel works well, so you can wrap twine around the other end.

5 Cut out a smaller shape from the storybook and stick this directly onto the parcel.

6 Wrap the parcel in striped twine. I like to wrap the twine just around the top of the parcel a few times, so that it doesn't cover any of the Christmas decoration. Tie in a knot at the back, but if you want to attach a luggage tag, do this before tying the knot. You can also attach the luggage tag simply by slipping it under the twine, or add a splash more colour by attaching it with a piece of washi tape.

PINE-NEEDLE TASSELS

This is a lovely way to incorporate traditional Christmas foliage into your wrapping. If you can't find pine needles, just use sprigs of Christmas-tree branches (save a few branches in a jug of water when you put up your tree). These need to be made as close as possible to handing out your gift, preferably not more than two days in advance.

WHAT TO DO

① Take a bundle of pine needles and arrange them so they are all the same length. Trim the bottom tips (the ends that were attached to the tree) to neaten them if necessary. It's fine if there's a mixture of needles still attached in clumps and individual needles. If you are using sprigs of Christmas-tree branch, cut the branches to lengths of about 12 cm (5 in).

② Wrap coloured twine several times around the pine needles (or branches) about 2 cm (¾ in) from their ends and secure the bundle with a knot, leaving a sufficient length of twine to wrap around your present.

③ Wrap your gift (plain-coloured wrapping paper will show off your pine-needle tassel to greatest effect).

④ Thread the gift tag onto the twine so it's near the tassel, then wrap the excess twine around your gift, ensuring the tassel is sitting on top. Tie the twine in a knot at the back of the gift.

YOU WILL NEED:

▼ pine needles (or sprigs of fresh Christmas-tree branch)

▼ scissors (optional)

▼ coloured twine

▼ plain-coloured wrapping paper

▼ sticky tape (Scotch tape)

▼ gift tags

SPOON GIFT TAGS

These are particularly good if your gift is food related, such as a cookbook or a cooking ingredient or equipment. But whatever the gift, they're fun to make and will no doubt make the recipient smile.

WHAT TO DO

1 The spoons used as gift tags can be attached to your gift either by making a hole in their end and threading twine through the hole to wrap around the gift, or by simply tucking the spoons into the twine. If making a hole, use a metal skewer to make a hole in the handle end of the spoon, ensuring it's large enough to thread twine or ribbon through.

2 There are two ways to paint the ends of the spoons. The first way is to dip the handles into the paint pots about a quarter of the way up the spoon. Allow any excess paint to drip off, then, if you've made a hole, use a wooden skewer to open up the hole. Leave to dry, sitting across the top of a cup or similar with newspaper underneath it. Alternatively, if using tubes of paint, squeeze a little into a small pot and paint the spoon end using the paintbrush. (Doing this on an angle looks effective.) Skewer and dry as above.

3 Alternatively, decorate the ends of the spoons with washi tape. Simply wrap one or two strips of tape around the bottom of each spoon, then, if you've made a hole, stick a skewer through the tape to open up the hole.

4 Write the gift recipient's name in the concave part of the spoon using black texta. You can also write who it is from on the back of the spoon.

5 Wrap your gift and then tie on the spoon. I like to wrap the twine around the gift a few times, so I use a long length of twine. To do this, wrap the twine three times around one end of the gift, about a quarter of the way along the gift so there's room for the spoon to dangle. On the last loop, thread the spoon onto the twine, then tie the twine in a knot at the back. The spoon tag will be able to move along the twine, so ensure it is sitting at the front of the gift. If you didn't make a hole in the spoon, just tuck it into the twine or ribbon (if using this method, ensure the twine is tied quite tightly so the spoon stays in place).

YOU WILL NEED:

▼ metal skewer (optional)

▼ bamboo spoons (1 per gift)

▼ small amount of paint in the colour of your choice

▼ paint pots

▼ wooden skewer (optional)

▼ cup

newspaper

▼ paintbrush (if using tubes of paint rather than pots)

▼ washi tape (optional)

▼ black texta (marker pen)

wrapping paper

▼ sticky tape (Scotch tape)

▼ twine or ribbon

57

LAYERED WRAPPING WITH BUTTONS

*Create layers of different textures and end with a few buttons–
simple but fun. Use buttons with holes that aren't too tiny,
otherwise you won't be able to thread the twine through.*

WHAT TO DO

1 Wrap your present in the textured white paper, keeping the joins neat and any folds crisp.

2 Cut a strip of coloured paper, making it about half the width of your gift and long enough to wrap all the way around the gift. If you have a lovely piece of paper that you want to use but it doesn't go all the way around, that's fine: it just needs to be long enough to cover the front of the gift and two sides. Wrap the strip around the gift, securing it at the back with sticky tape.

3 Wrap string or twine around the gift a couple of times, either in the same direction as the coloured paper or at right angles to it. You can skip the next step of adding buttons to the twine if you like (as in the top example pictured opposite); if you do, simply tie the twine in a neat bow on top of the present. If you'd like to add buttons, leave the twine untied on top of the gift for now.

4 To add buttons, simply thread the string through some buttons (five to six for a large gift, three or four for a smaller one). You will probably need to do this without a needle, as most twines are too thick for a needle. If you find a needle with a wide enough eye, it will probably then be too thick to go through the buttonholes! However, if you do find the perfect combination, by all means use a needle, as it will save time.

5 Make sure the buttons are sitting nice and flat on top of the gift, then wrap the string (without any buttons on it) underneath the gift and tie in a neat knot.

6 Tie a luggage tag onto the gift, if desired.

YOU WILL NEED:

▼ textured white paper

▼ sticky tape (Scotch tape)

▼ scissors

▼ coloured paper, such as wrapping paper or crepe paper

▼ rustic string or twine

▼ buttons (optional)

▼ luggage tags (optional)

CONTRASTING WRAPPING

Most people have the ends of wrapping paper rolls hanging around and this is an ideal way to use these bits up. Alternatively, you can plan your design and buy two contrasting rolls of paper. I like to do one plain colour and one patterned, but it's completely up to you.

YOU WILL NEED:

▼ **two contrasting wrapping papers**

▼ **sticky tape (Scotch tape)**

▼ **washi tape (optional)**

▼ **coloured twine or rustic string (optional)**

WHAT TO DO

1 Plan how you are going to wrap your gift. For example, will one wrapping paper cover half the gift, the other paper, the other half? Or will you use one paper for a quarter of the gift and the other one to cover the other three-quarters? Will you wrap on an angle or in straight lines? Decide before you start.

2 Once you've worked out your design, take the first piece of paper and wrap the entire gift as you would normally, securing the joins with sticky tape.

3 Take the second piece of paper and fold about 1 cm (½ in) of one edge under. Make sure this is the edge that meets the other piece of paper so that there's a nice neat finish. Wrap the gift according to your design, securing with either sticky tape or washi tape.

4 If one of the pieces of paper used is plain coloured, you can add a few strips of washi tape to this piece if you like (just for fun!).

5 It's up to you if you add any twine to this wrapping or not. If you do, keep it simple with just one loop around the gift, otherwise it can start to look too busy. Tie the twine in a neat knot at the back.

GIFT BAGS

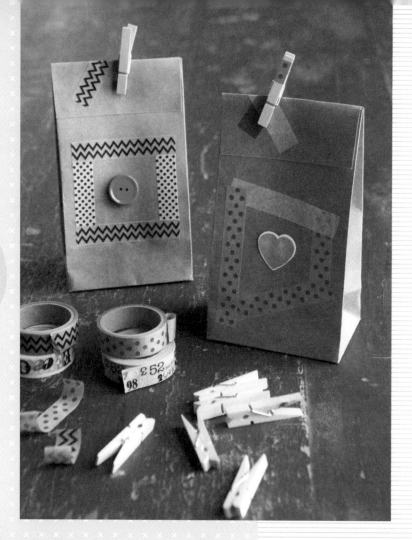

Small items like jewellery can be fiddly to wrap and make look beautiful if you don't have a box. These craft-type gift bags solve this problem. How you embellish your bag is up to you.

WHAT TO DO

1. Lie each bag flat and create a 'frame' using washi tape (see the photo for ideas).

2. Using craft glue, stick a button into the middle of the frame (make sure the buttons have a flat base, otherwise they won't stick). You can also use stickers of your choice to decorate the inside of the frames.

3. Pop your gift into the bag, fold the top of the bag over and clip the bag closed using a small wooden peg.

4. Decorate the folded-over top of the bag with a strip of washi tape, too, if desired.

YOU WILL NEED:

▼ brown craft or gift bags

▼ washi tape

▼ craft glue

▼ buttons and/or stickers of your choice

▼ small wooden pegs (available from craft shops)

CELEBRATIONS

Champagne cocktails

Prawns with tomato & basil
vinaigrette

Grilled salmon with miso glaze

Lemon & lime tartlets

Wedding cake

Petits fours & coffee

Table 3

mr + Mrs

WEDDINGS

Planning the style or theme of your wedding can be quite stressful when you first start thinking about it. However, it really is possible – and enjoyable – to create a lot of your wedding yourself by keeping to a central theme. In this chapter I've suggested two themes: the first is based on the happy couple's initials and a love heart (i.e. K ♥ A), and the second is a classic black-and-white theme. There are also various other ideas to inspire you, which can be incorporated into most styles of wedding.

One word of advice: if you plan to make a lot of these projects, allow yourself plenty of time and consider asking a few friends or family members to help. Have everything you are going to need ready beforehand, and be methodical in your planning and creating. I did much of the styling for my own wedding and have fond memories, not only of the wedding day itself, but also of the weeks beforehand, which I spent sourcing items and painting 100 place-setting stones with a friend!

PHOTO-BOOTH FRAME

As well as the official wedding photos, it's lovely to have some more casual ones of the guests enjoying the big day. This photo-booth frame idea creates a place for them to take some fun shots.

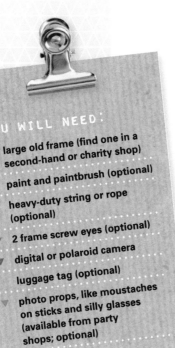

YOU WILL NEED:

- ▼ large old frame (find one in a second-hand or charity shop)
- ▼ paint and paintbrush (optional)
- ▼ heavy-duty string or rope (optional)
- ▼ 2 frame screw eyes (optional)
- ▼ digital or polaroid camera
- ▼ luggage tag (optional)
- ▼ photo props, like moustaches on sticks and silly glasses (available from party shops; optional)

WHAT TO DO

1. If painting the frame, paint it well in advance so it is dry! Paint it either white or in a colour to match the theme of the wedding. If it's a gorgeous frame already, leave it as is.

2. You can either place your frame on a table so guests can simply pick it up and hold it for their photo, or attach some heavy-duty string or rope to the frame so you can hang it somewhere. Do this by attaching a couple of strong screw eyes to the back top corners of the frame and threading the string through these, ensuring the knots are pulled nice and tight (the length of the string required will depend on how low you want the frame to hang).

3. If hanging the frame, hang it in a pretty place, e.g. from a tree in a garden, or somewhere with a plain background.

4. Leave your camera there so guests can take photos of themselves behind the frame. You may want to attach a luggage tag to the camera to remind people to leave the camera there for others to take photos with, so no-one wanders off with it!

5. If you want some slightly sillier photos, leave some props there too for your guests to use (e.g. moustaches on sticks, silly glasses etc).

GUEST MESSAGE BOOK

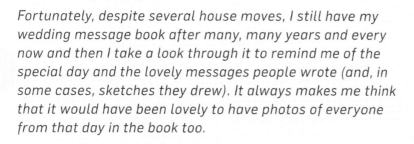

Fortunately, despite several house moves, I still have my wedding message book after many, many years and every now and then I take a look through it to remind me of the special day and the lovely messages people wrote (and, in some cases, sketches they drew). It always makes me think that it would have been lovely to have photos of everyone from that day in the book too.

WHAT TO DO

1. Set aside a table especially for your message book. Place it and a beautiful pen on the table along with a polaroid camera and some double-sided tape.
2. Direct your guests to the table and encourage them to take a quick snap of themselves and stick it in the book along with their message.

YOU WILL NEED:
- beautiful notebook
- pen (make it a lovely one)
- polaroid camera
- double-sided tape

TABLE DECORATIONS

All of the following projects can be used either as table number decorations or as name place settings. (The number of wedding guests may determine whether it is practical to use them as name place settings.)

CANDLE-LIGHT JARS

WHAT TO DO

1. Cut pieces of lightweight craft paper to fit snugly inside the jars (check step 2 before doing this if you'd like to print your table numbers). Alternatively tear the paper so the torn edges produce a softer look.

2. Write, paint or print each table number (or guest's name) onto the middle of one side of the paper. If painting, allow the number to dry completely before doing step 3. If printing, ensure your printer can print on the size of paper you're using – some printers can't print on small pieces of paper, so you may need to first print on an A4 sheet and then cut it to size.

3. Put the paper inside each of the jars, ensuring the table number is clearly visible. Add one large or a couple of small battery-operated tea lights (don't use real candles as the paper could catch on fire).

YOU WILL NEED:

- scissors
- lightweight, slightly see-through craft paper, in the colour of your choice
- large glass jars
- texta (marker pen) or paint and small paintbrush or printer
- battery-operated LED tea lights (at least 1 per jar)

CUP AND FORK PLACE SETTINGS

WHAT TO DO

1. The name tags for these place settings are each about 1½ cm x 9 cm (½ in x 3½ in). If you are going to write the names, cut the card into pieces with these dimensions and write the names on with the texta. If printing the names on the card, plan the layout on your computer, then type all the names and print them off on the card. Neatly cut out the names as above.

2. To make the chevron at one end of the name tag, measure 1 cm (about ½ in) in from the end and make a dot at this point in the middle of the tag. Cut to the dot from both corners to form the chevron shape.

3. Cut pieces of the florist foam to fit snugly inside the cups, leaving about a 1–2 cm (½–1 in) gap at the top. Put a piece of foam into each cup.

4. Carefully slot each card through the tines of the forks.

5. Press the handle end of each fork into the florist foam, pushing it all the way down to make it stable.

6. Cover the exposed foam in the cup with small buttons or pebbles.

YOU WILL NEED

- scissors
- ruler
- 1 or 2 sheets of A4 card (depending on how many guests you have), in the colour of your choice
- texta (marker pen), in the colour of your choice, or printer
- florist foam
- small white ceramic cups without handles
- old forks
- small white buttons or small white pebbles

SUCCULENTS IN A FLOWERPOT

YOU WILL NEED

▼ small terracotta flowerpots
▼ coloured paint (optional)
▼ small paintbrush
▼ black or white paint
▼ paper (optional)
▼ succulent soil
▼ succulents
▼ small white pebbles

WHAT TO DO

1. Depending on the style of the wedding, either leave the pots their original terracotta colour or paint them to match the theme of the wedding. If painting them, leave to dry completely.

2. Next paint table numbers or guests' names in black or white on each pot. (You might want to practise this on paper first.) If you want the numbers/names to look a little stylised, check out some different fonts on your computer and try copying one that you like.

3. Half fill each flowerpot with soil suitable for your chosen succulent(s) and add one or two plants to each pot. Add a bit more soil, pressing it down quite firmly and leaving at least a 1 cm (½ in) gap at the top. Add enough water to moisten the soil, but don't flood it.

4. Arrange the white pebbles on top of the soil.

5. If using as name place settings, give the flowerpots to your guests as wedding favours at the end of the big day.

KIDS' TABLE

Keep the kids happy at the wedding by giving them their own table and some things to do while the speeches are happening.

IDEAS TO KEEP THE KIDS HAPPY AND OCCUPIED:

▼ Instead of glasses, give each child a small bottle to drink out of. Wrap each bottle in a small piece of coloured paper and secure by tying pretty twine around the bottle a few times. Add a stripey or spotty straw and tuck a flag (*see* p. 103 for ideas) with each child's name on it into the twine. Alternatively put a frame sticker onto each bottle and write each child's name inside the frame. Add a stripey or spotty straw.

▼ Fill small jars with Smarties or mini marshmallows. Write each child's name on a luggage tag and tie the tag around the neck of each jar with string or write each child's name on a pretty sticker and stick these on top of the jars.

▼ Wrap up crayons or colouring pencils in pretty paper (that matches the wedding theme) and leave one at each place setting.

▼ Print (or draw if you are artistic) an outline of a bride and groom onto A4 paper and get the kids to colour it in. You could also make cards with a bride and groom drawn on them and ask the children to colour them in and write you a wedding-day message.

▼ Here is a great activity if you only have a few kids coming. Provide the kids with scraps of material, glue and the outline of a bride and groom and get them to 'dress' the happy couple using the fabrics. You could also provide feathers, pompoms and sequins – the more sparkle the better!

K ♥ A
THEME

This is quite a simple theme that can be applied to any wedding. It uses the happy couple's first initials with a heart in between them.

INITIAL AND HEART PLACEMATS

You can use either linen or hessian for these romantic placemats. The stamping is done using potato stamps you make yourself – they are really easy to make. If you can find rubber stamps with your initials and a heart in the correct size, you could use these instead, if you prefer.

You could continue the theme and make matching napkins too, although I would recommend using linen or cotton rather than hessian for napkins.

WHAT TO DO

1. Cut the fabric into rectangles sized 42 cm x 31 cm (16½ in x 12 in). It's a good idea to check that your table is big enough for mats of this size, and resize them if necessary. Working on one rectangle at a time, fold over a 1 cm (½ in) hem on all sides and iron so there's a distinct hem.

2. Cut four lengths of no-sew hemming tape (the same lengths as the four sides of the placemat) and place one length inside the folded fabric of the hem. Put a clean damp cloth on top of the fabric and iron along the hem with a hot iron (do not use the steam setting). Repeat for the other three sides. (You can use a sewing machine for this step, if you have one.) If you are having a rustic wedding you could skip these two steps altogether and leave the edges unhemmed.

3. Work out what size you want the initials and heart to be (these initials are 5 cm x 5 cm/2 in x 2 in and the heart is 4 cm/1½ in high). Using a simple font that's thick enough to cut around, print the initials and the heart onto a piece of paper at your selected size. Carefully cut out the letters.

YOU WILL NEED:

- ▼ scissors
- ▼ linen, calico or hessian fabric (the amount you need will depend on how many placemats you are making; each mat is 42 cm x 31 cm/ 16½ in x 12 in)
- ▼ iron and ironing board
- ▼ no-sew hemming tape, about 0.75 cm (¼ in) wide, or sewing machine
- ▼ damp cloth
- ▼ printer and piece of paper
- ▼ 2 medium–large potatoes, peeled (big enough to fit the letters and heart shape)
- ▼ pen or sharp pencil
- ▼ small sharp knife
- ▼ newspaper
- ▼ fabric paint, in the colour of your choice
- ▼ small paintbrush
- ▼ paper to practise stamping

4. To make the stamps, slice one potato in half and put one of the cut-out paper initials in the middle of the cut side, putting it on the potato back-to-front so that it's the right way around when you stamp it. Draw around the initial with a pen or sharp pencil, including any inside detail, such as on an 'A'.

5. Remove the paper cut-out and carefully cut around the initial using a small sharp knife until you are left with the shape of the initial (*see* photo on p. 76).

6. Repeat steps 4 and 5 for the second initial and the heart.

7. Now comes the fun stamping part. Lay the first placemat on a sheet or two of newspaper. Put some fabric paint on a paintbrush and paint the first potato stamp's initial (i.e. in this case, the 'K'). Have a practice stamping on a piece of paper to ensure the initial stamps properly – you may need to shave a few ragged edges off.

8. Once you are happy with how the initial stamps, put some more paint onto the stamp and stamp the first placemat. (It works best if you stamp the initials down the right- or left-hand side of the placemat in a vertical line so that you can still see them when the crockery etc is in situ on the placemat.) Repeat this step, adding the first initial to the rest of the placemats, reapplying the paint for each one.

9. Repeat steps 7 and 8 with the heart and then the second initial. Leave the placemats to dry completely before using.

TABLE ALLOCATION CHALKBOARD

This project applies the heart theme to your table allocation board, with chalked initials and a heart at the top of the board and the lists of who's sitting at each table underneath.

You will need a piece of plywood 6 mm (¼ in) thick to make this. The other dimensions of the plywood will depend on the number of tables you're going to have; the list of names for each table will most likely fit on a piece of card or paper that's A5 in size or smaller. You also need to allow for extra space at the top of the chalkboard for your initials and a heart along with a bit of space at the bottom. (This board is 45 cm x 60 cm/18 in x 24 in.)

If you have amazing writing, a very steady hand and not too many guests, you could attempt to write all the names on the chalkboard, instead of printing them out onto the A5 sheets. However, if you do this I suggest using a 'chalk pen' (available from craft shops) rather than chalk, otherwise you may end up with lots of smudges.

WHAT TO DO

1. Ensure the plywood is clean (there is no need to sand it). Using the chalkboard paint and a roller brush, paint one side of the board and allow to dry completely. Give a second coat of paint and leave to dry completely.

2. Print off each table's guest list on A5 sheets of card or paper (or smaller, depending on the size of your board and how many tables you have), choosing a font that is suitably celebratory. You can include table numbers on the printed cards or leave them off and make them part of the design on your chalkboard.

3. Once the paint is completely dry, you can start chalking. You will probably want to do a rough plan beforehand, as, although you can wash off the chalk, it can start to look a little messy if too many mistakes are made. Start from the top and work down, so you aren't rubbing the chalk with your hand as you go. At the top of the chalkboard, do a rough outline of the heart and the happy couple's first initials (e.g. K ♥ A) with chalk and, once you're happy, colour it in. Any straight lines should be drawn using a ruler to keep everything looking nice and neat.

4. Once the top part is done, take the chalkboard outside and blow hard over it a couple of times to remove any chalk dust.

5. Next draw outlines on the chalkboard for each table's guest list (i.e. the ones on the A5 cards) using a ruler not only to ensure straight lines, but to ensure the outlines are all the same size, i.e. slightly larger than the size of the A5 cards so as to form a frame around the cards. If you are also chalking on table numbers, do this now too.

6. Starting from the top left, stick your printed table guest lists onto the chalkboard in their allocated spots, using either double-sided tape or Blu Tack.

▼ piece of plywood
(see above for size)

▼ chalkboard paint

▼ roller brush and paint tray

A5 card or paper

▼ chalk

ruler

▼ double-sided tape
or Blu Tack

OTHER IDEAS FOR YOUR CHALKBOARD:

▼ If you have space, you could chalk on extra hearts or initials.

▼ Add sweet words like 'Mr & Mrs' or 'Happily Ever After'.

▼ Chalk the date of your wedding at the bottom.

▼ Stick on a black-and-white photo of the happy couple with Blu Tack.

K ♥ A

menu

Champagne bellini
Oysters with ginger & lemongrass
Rare roast beef with Sichuan pepper crust
Summer fruit tartlets with crème Anglaise

Chocolate wedding cake
Petits fours & coffee

K ♥ A

I ♥ YOU MENU

Using a program on your computer, such as Publisher or InDesign, create your menus following the initials and heart theme, using the photo on this page as a guide. Print the menu off onto A5 cards in your colour of choice.

LOLLY JAR PLACE SETTINGS
AND TAKE-HOME FAVOURS

These are lovely take-home gifts for wedding guests. If you are having a small wedding or have lots of time beforehand, you could paint the initials and heart in silver or gold paint using stencils, rather than stamping them.

WHAT TO DO

1. Cut strips of linen about 4–5 cm (1½ –2 in) wide and long enough to wrap around the jars with a 1 cm (½ in) overlap.

2. Using the stamps and ink pad, stamp the bride's and groom's first initials and the heart onto the middle section of each piece of linen, e.g. K ♥ A.

3. Using glue or double-sided tape, stick one end of the linen piece to the jar. Wrap it around the middle of the jar and secure the other end with more glue or tape.

4. Write each guest's name on a luggage tag with texta.

5. Fill each jar with jelly beans, marshmallows etc (or your choice of filling), pop the lid on securely and tie a luggage tag around the neck of each jar with string or twine. You can also wrap a piece of string around the linen piece, if you like, tying a knot to secure it.

6. Put a lolly jar at each place setting, reminding everyone to take them home as wedding favours.

YOU WILL NEED

▼ linen (or your choice of fabric to match the wedding)

▼ small stamps (about 1 cm/ ½ in) of bride's and groom's first initials and heart stamp

▼ ink pad

▼ glue or double-sided tape

▼ small jars with lids (1 for each guest)

▼ luggage tags

▼ texta (marker pen)

▼ jelly beans, marshmallows, silver dragees, amaretti biscuits etc to fill the jars

▼ string or twine

A black-and-white theme looks classy, simple and clean. I've made a few suggestions on what to theme black and white, but you could take it further with the flowers and other decorations.

SIMPLE
BLACK-AND-
WHITE THEME

FRAME SEATING-ALLOCATION BOARD

In the lead-up to the wedding, look out for old picture frames in second-hand shops, charity shops and on internet sites. The size the frame needs to be will depend on how many tables there will be at the wedding. The frame I used is approximately 60 cm x 70 cm (23½ in x 27½ in).

WHAT TO DO

1. Clean the frame and sand any rough bits, then paint it white. You can either use normal paint or spray-paint; spray-paint is quicker, but it's up to you. If you do use spray-paint, make sure you're in a well-ventilated space, preferably outdoors. It will probably need a couple of coats. Allow to dry completely.

2. Cut the sheet of cardboard so that it fits exactly into the back of the frame or sits on the border of the frame. Attach it to the frame using masking tape or glue.

3. Next you need to create the guest lists for each table; these will be attached within the frame. Work out how many tables there are going to be at the wedding and calculate what size each piece of paper (with the guest lists written on them) needs to be, in order to fit within the frame. Cut the cardboard or craft paper to this size. Alternatively you may need to print out your guest list first and then cut to size.

4. Type up the guest list for each table, including table number and guest names, and print each one out on the cardboard or craft paper.

5. Depending on the look of the wedding, stick the guest lists to the cardboard within the frame with washi tape, pins or double-sided tape.

YOU WILL NEED

- ▼ large frame
- ▼ sandpaper
- ▼ paintbrush
- ▼ white paint or spray-paint
- ▼ scissors
- ▼ sheet of cardboard just larger than the inside of the frame
- ▼ masking tape or glue
- ▼ cardboard or craft paper (thin enough to go through a printer)
- ▼ black-and-white washi tape, pins or double-sided tape

- ▼ newspaper
- ▼ several branches (1 per vase), about 60–70 cm (24–28 in) tall
- ▼ white spray-paint
- ▼ several narrow-necked white vases or jars (1 per table)
- ▼ printer or thick black texta (marker pen) or black paint and paintbrush
- ▼ white heart-shaped gift tags or white cards, each about 15 cm x 10 cm (6 in x 4 in)
- ▼ scissors
- ▼ hole puncher
- ▼ black ribbon
- ▼ wedding menu printed onto pieces of white card, each about 9 cm x 13 cm (3½ in x 5 in)
- ▼ black-and-white hanging heart decorations (optional)

TABLE CENTREPIECE

Either ask your florist for the branches or sprays used in this project, or find them yourself beforehand.

For extra fun you could write cute messages on cardboard love hearts and also hang these from the branches. Messages such as 'Mr & Mrs', 'Happily ever after' and 'You are my sunshine' are fun, or personalise them with things that are special to the happy couple.

WHAT TO DO

1. Spread several sheets of newspaper outside and spray-paint the branches with the white paint. Ensure each branch is well covered. Leave to dry completely.

2. Put a branch into each vase.

3. Print out, write or paint the table numbers onto the gift tags or pieces of white card. If using cards, cut these out to form heart shapes (you can find in the free clip-art on your computer if you wish) around the table number.

4. Punch a single hole in the top of each table-number love-heart card. Cut lengths of black ribbon about 12 cm (5 in) long and thread through each hole. Tie a knot in the ribbon near the hole to secure.

5. Punch a hole in the top of each wedding-menu card and thread black ribbon through these too, securing with a knot.

6. Tie a menu and table number onto the branch in each vase. If desired, you could also add several hanging heart decorations to each branch.

GLOSSY NAME SETTINGS

Paint stones or pebbles with high-gloss white spray-paint (in a well-ventilated space, preferably outdoors). Leave them to dry completely, then, using a good-quality black texta (marker pen), write a guest's name onto each stone. Set the table with white crockery and black napery, and place the name-setting stones on the black napkins for contrast.

PARTIES AND DINNER PARTIES

I love having friends around for dinner. Now that I have kids I don't have as much time to prepare an elaborate meal as I used to, but I still want to socialise with my friends at home, so these days I tend to keep the food more simple (and often make dishes that can be prepared ahead) and spend time ensuring the table looks beautiful or stylish or fun, depending on the occasion.

This chapter shows you how to create a simple Asian-themed table (you could even do this and then order takeaway!); a fun 'disposable' party, where you can let your creative side run wild; and a beautiful table styled with masses of flowers (this theme works equally well inside or out, but particularly for a dinner held outside at dusk and then into the night). These are just ideas, so feel free to take the ideas and make them work for your own theme.

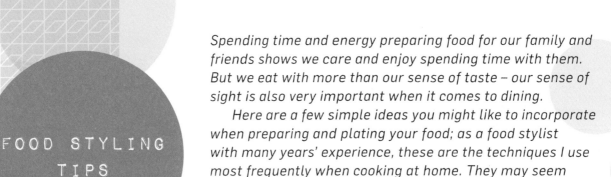

FOOD STYLING TIPS

Spending time and energy preparing food for our family and friends shows we care and enjoy spending time with them. But we eat with more than our sense of taste – our sense of sight is also very important when it comes to dining.

Here are a few simple ideas you might like to incorporate when preparing and plating your food; as a food stylist with many years' experience, these are the techniques I use most frequently when cooking at home. They may seem unimportant, but it's often what isn't noticed rather than what is that counts.

▼ When slicing vegetables slice them on the diagonal. This makes them look more attractive than if there are blunt ends. Even if you are just cutting the ends off green beans, cut them on a diagonal.

▼ When slicing onions and shallots, don't just chop off the top and bottom, as this makes the ends of the slices blunt. Instead, peel the onion, then cut it in half from top to bottom. Sit the onion flat and slice it across-ways from top to bottom to give what I call 'toenail' shaped pieces. If you leave the tips on onions and shallots when cooking them whole or in halves, you end up with a much prettier shape.

▼ If you are making a delicate salad, use a mandolin to slice radishes, cucumber etc very thinly. They will look far prettier than chunks or thick slices. However, if the rest of the salad is chunky, then it will look better if the vegetables are cut into chunky pieces too.

▼ I'm not into restaurant-type styling, i.e. dots and smears, but when plating your food take care with how it is arranged and use a piece of paper towel to wipe away any splashes of sauce or gravy.

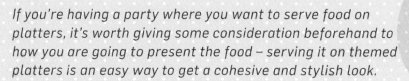

STYLING PLATTERS

YOU WILL NEED:

- ▼ piece of plywood about 60 cm x 45 cm (24 in x 18 in) and 6 mm (¼ in) thick
- ▼ black chalkboard paint
- ▼ paint tray
- ▼ small roller brush
- ▼ chalk
- ▼ ruler
- ▼ baking paper
- ▼ sticky tape (Scotch tape; optional)

If you're having a party where you want to serve food on platters, it's worth giving some consideration beforehand to how you are going to present the food – serving it on themed platters is an easy way to get a cohesive and stylish look.

CHALKBOARDS

You can do whatever you like with these chalkboard platters. It will depend on what you are serving or what your theme is as to what you chalk on them. I love to do a cheese board this way, or if I'm having a drinks party, I often prepare a load of ham-and-cheese rolls to serve at around midnight to soak up the alcohol.

It's up to you whether you paint one or both sides of the board. The advantage of painting both is that you can use both sides during the evening without having to remove the chalk completely each time.

WHAT TO DO

1. Ensure the plywood is clean (there is no need to sand it).

2. If painting both sides of the board it's easiest to complete one side at a time. Pour some black chalkboard paint into the paint tray and, using the roller brush, apply the paint to the plywood. Each side will need two coats of paint (allow to dry in between coats). Using a roller brush rather than a paintbrush gives a smoother finish.

3. Once the paint is completely dry, the fun part of designing your board starts. You can do whatever you like, but if going with the cheese-platter idea, draw on the outline of a cheese board with the chalk and then write the names of each cheese close to the spots where the cheese will be sitting. For the ham-and-cheese rolls idea, draw around the outside of a plate onto the chalkboard, then around another larger plate (so you end up with two circles, one inside the other) and then write a fun message on the bottom of the board, such as 'Yum Yum!', 'Oooh, Looks Good' or 'Grub's Up'. When drawing on your board, use a ruler for any lines that need to be straight.

4. Once you have your drawing and any words in place, take the chalkboard outside and blow hard on it a couple of times to remove any chalk dust. This also makes the lines stand out more.

5. If going with the cheese-platter idea, sit each piece of cheese on individual pieces of baking paper, ensuring you don't cover up any of the words. For the ham-and-cheese rolls, wrap a strip of baking paper around each roll, secure with sticky tape and pile them onto the board just before serving.

OLD BOARDS

Old breadboards, pizza paddles and the like are a great way to serve food –
the bigger they are, the more drama they add to the occasion. You can simply
put your food directly on the board, or incorporate some baking paper for
more detail, texture and an extra rustic touch. Tear off a piece of baking paper
just a little smaller than your board then scrunch it up. Un-scrunch it, put it on
the board and then sit the food on top of this.

BOARDS, PLATTERS AND PLATES WITH BANANA LEAVES

This is a good way to give a cohesive look to platters of food if you don't have lots of crockery that matches. Banana leaves are available from Asian supermarkets (or the banana tree in your garden if you are lucky enough to have one). Cut or tear pieces of leaves to fit your boards, plates and platters; you can either cut the leaves to fit snugly on the platters or leave the ends hanging over the edges.

FLAGS AND TOPPERS

Let your imagination run wild with these fun decorations. The flags can be used either to let your guests know what you are serving or just for silly or celebratory messages. If you have good hand-writing, simply write your messages on the flags; alternatively choose a fun font on your computer then print off messages and stick them on the flags.

FLAGS

There are two ways to make these flags: as a simple rectangle of paper taped to a toothpick or as a flag with a classic chevron end (like an inverted 'V').

WHAT TO DO

Method 1: Simple

YOU WILL NEED:

▼ printer and paper or thin cardboard

▼ scissors

▼ black or coloured texta (marker pen; optional)

▼ sticky tape (Scotch tape)

▼ toothpicks (1 per flag)

1 If printing off your message, type it up on the computer using your favourite font (ensuring it is the correct size to fit on the cardboard), then print it out either on thin cardboard or paper if the board is too thick.

2 Cut the card into rectangles about 9 cm x 2 cm (3½ in x ¾ in). If writing your messages, simply cut the card into rectangles then write the messages.

3 Tape a toothpick to the middle and back of each rectangle.

4 Once your food is in place on the board, platter or plate, stick a few flags in the top of some of the food.

Method 2: Chevron

1 If printing off your message, type it up on the computer using your favourite font. Space the messages to ensure they will sit on the right side of the rectangle only, as the flags are folded in half (see measurement following). Print the messages out either on thin cardboard or paper if your board is too thick to go through the printer.

2 Cut the card (or paper) into rectangles about 16 cm x 2 cm (6 in x ¾ in). If using paper, glue the messages onto the cardboard rectangles. Bend each rectangle in half exactly.

3 If writing your messages, cut and fold first, then write your messages using black or coloured texta; you can write on one or both sides.

YOU WILL NEED:

▼ printer and paper or thin cardboard

▼ scissors

▼ craft glue

▼ black or coloured texta (marker pen)

▼ toothpicks (1 per flag)

4 Open up the folded rectangle and put glue on the side without writing on it. Put a toothpick in the fold (to act as the 'flagpole') then stick the two halves together.

5 Once the glue has dried, cut a chevron shape out of the flag ends. To do this, measure 1 cm (½ in) in from the end and make a dot at this point in the middle of the flag. Cut to the dot from both corners to form the chevron ('V') shape.

6 Once your food is in place on the board, platter or plate, stick a few flags in the top of some of the food.

FIREWORK TOPPERS

These are a fun idea that I like to do for celebrations like New Year's Eve. I like to think of them as indoor fireworks! Stick them into food to add a bit of sparkle and colour.

WHAT TO DO

1. Start by drawing several triangles (one triangle for each topper you're making) with curved bottoms onto the cardboard. Make each triangle about 8 cm (3 in) across the base and 4 cm (1½ in) on each side.

2. Cut the triangles out, ensuring you make the bottoms slightly curved. Fold each triangle in half.

3. Cut pieces of crepe paper into roughly 4½ cm (2 in) squares. Fold each piece in half and then in half again in the same direction, so you end up with a long, thin shape.

4. Cut several long slits into each piece of crepe paper, stopping just short of the top.

5. Using sticky tape, tape the uncut end of each piece of crepe paper to the top of a toothpick (or skewer if you prefer longer toppers), wrapping the tape around the toothpick a few times.

6. Open up each triangle of cardboard and place a toothpick down the middle of the triangle, so the crepe paper sticks out the top (ensuring you can't see the sticky tape). Don't sit the toothpick in the fold, otherwise you'll end up with a wonky topper! (You can stick the toothpick in place with a small piece of sticky tape before gluing the two sides of the triangle together, but this isn't vital.)

7. Glue the two sides of the cardboard triangle together. Gently loosen the crepe paper so that it splays out like fireworks.

YOU WILL NEED:
- pencil
- sheet of sparkly or coloured cardboard
- scissors
- crepe paper
- sticky tape (Scotch tape)
- toothpicks or skewers (1 per topper)
- craft glue

ASIAN THEME – BLACK, WHITE AND RED

It's pretty simple to create an Asian theme for your table. Stick with black, red and white as your colour scheme and your dinner table will look striking.

RED NAPKINS

If you don't already have red napkins and don't want the expense of buying new ones, buy some red tea towels (these are usually much cheaper) and cut them into napkins.

WHAT TO DO

1 Cut each tea towel into rectangles about 50 cm x 40 cm (20 in x 16 in).

2 Working on one rectangle at a time, fold over a 1 cm (½ in) hem on all sides and iron so you have a distinct hem. Cut four lengths of no-sew tape (2 x 50 cm/20 in, and 2 x 40 cm/16 in) and place one length inside the folded fabric of the hem (i.e. 50 cm/20 in length for the corresponding length of the napkin and so on). Put a clean, damp dishcloth on top of the fabric and iron along the hem with a hot iron (do not use the steam setting). Repeat for the other three sides. (You can use a sewing machine for this step, if you have one.)

3 Iron your new 'napkins'.

YOU WILL NEED:

- **scissors**
- ▼ **sheets from an Asian newspaper (available from Asian grocers and supermarkets)**
- ▼ **battery-operated LED tea lights**
- **red or black washi tape**

ASIAN TEA LIGHTS

Tea lights add instant atmosphere to a dinner table. These simple ones are wrapped in Asian newspaper and look very effective.

WHAT TO DO

1. Cut strips from an Asian newspaper about 13 cm (5 in) long (or as long as the circumference of your tea lights) and 3½ cm (1½ in) high.
2. Wrap the strips around the tea lights, then secure the join with a piece of washi tape, tucking it over the top for neatness.

CHOPSTICK RESTS

These red-and-black pebble chopstick rests provide a striking look to an Asian-themed table. Try to match them with either black or red chopsticks or a combination of both.

WHAT TO DO

1. Wrap masking tape around the middle of each pebble, i.e. so that it's on the front and back of the pebble.
2. Paint half of each pebble with two coats of black paint, allowing to dry in between coats.
3. Once completely dry, remove the tape and put another strip of masking tape around each pebble, so that the unpainted half remains uncovered. Place the tape exactly along the line of the black paint to ensure a perfect line between the two colours.
4. Paint the other half of the pebbles with the red paint, again applying two coats and allowing to dry in between coats.
5. Once the paint is completely dry, carefully peel off the tape, ensuring none of the black paint peels off as you go.
6. Arrange the chopstick rests on your table, leaning red and/or black chopsticks on them.

YOU WILL NEED:

▼ masking tape
▼ pebbles (1 per guest)
▼ paintbrush
▼ black paint
▼ red paint

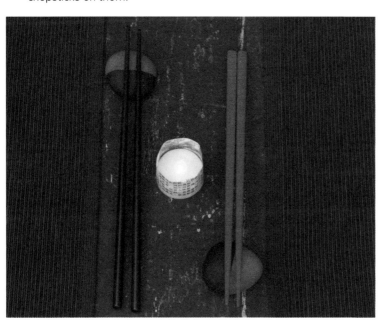

STYLING THE TABLE

To complete your Asian-themed dinner table, try to find some lanterns in an Asian supermarket or discount store and hang these close by. Add black placemats, some Asian crockery and some red tassels (available from craft or Asian shops). You could also serve one of the courses in noodle boxes for a bit of fun. To enhance the napkins, put a piece of gold-leaf style paper (available from Asian stores) on top of each one.

PAPER / DISPOSABLE THEME

Trends change so fast, sometimes it's hard to keep up. One way to avoid getting bored with tablecloths or placemats is to simply create your own from paper! You can be as creative as you like – and at the end of the meal why not invite your friends to add to your designs?

DECORATED PAPER TABLECLOTH

A great way to build on this theme is to write a few trivia questions on the paper tablecloth for guests to answer during the evening. Or write quotes or words related to a theme (e.g. Christmas, a birthday and so on) directly onto the tablecloth.

WHAT TO DO

1. Cover your table with the roll of paper; depending on the width of the table, you might need to use two long strips of paper. It is preferable to have about 15 cm (6 in) hanging down at either end, although it's not vital to have an overhang.

2. Clip a trouser hanger onto each end of the paper to help keep the paper in place while you draw on it.

3. Plan out your table design before you start, as you can't correct your mistakes! Using a black or coloured texta, draw a place setting outline for each guest, perhaps including a plate, cutlery and drink coaster. You can either draw freehand or trace around plates and bowls etc. Write the name of each guest inside the main dinner plate outline.

4. Leave each place setting simply as an outline, or get creative and decorate inside the lines with patterns such as zigzags, spots or swirls, or write the menu inside each 'plate'. You could also write a few inspirational quotes on the table and leave textas for your guests to add their own messages and drawings.

5. Don't forget to remove the trouser hangers before your guests arrive!

YOU WILL NEED:

- roll of brown paper (rolls are better than sheets as the paper doesn't have creases in it)
- 2 trouser hangers (the type with 2 clips on it)
- black or coloured texta (marker pen)
- assorted textas (marker pens; optional)

BAMBOO CUTLERY

Bamboo cutlery is becoming much easier to buy; most party shops now stock it. Although there is something beautiful about the plain bamboo, I like to add a bit of decoration to mine.

WHAT TO DO

1. Using the paintbrush, paint the handles of the cutlery pieces (about a third of the way up the handle). I like to do mine so you can see the brush marks where the painting ends. Alternatively put some paint in the paint pot and dip the handle of each piece into the pot about a third of the way up the handle, allowing any excess paint to drip off.

2. Leave to dry, sitting each piece across the top of a cup or similar, with newspaper underneath it.

3. Repeat steps 1 and 2 at least twice, and ensure the paint is completely dry before using the cutlery.

4. You can also decorate the cutlery with washi tape. To do this, cut strips of washi tape just long enough to wrap around the cutlery handles. Stick one or two pieces around the base of each handle, ensuring the joins are on the back.

YOU WILL NEED:

- bamboo cutlery (1 set per guest)
- paintbrush
- small amount of paint in the colour of your choice
- paint pot (optional)
- cup
- newspaper
- scissors
- washi tape

BAMBOO PLATES

You can find bamboo plates (and bowls etc) in party shops and gift shops. The great thing about buying plain bamboo plates is that you are free to adorn them with your own personalised messages and/or drawings.

You can choose to keep them plain and simple, of course, or get as creative as you like, adding words, pictures or quotes to the plates using typography stamps and an ink pad, or stencils. You can even work freehand if you're confident with your hand-writing and/or drawing abilities. To avoid any problems with ink etc leaching into the food, make sure you decorate only the rim.

You could write things like 'Yum!', 'Here Comes Dinner' or 'Happy Birthday Fred!', or even food-related quotes or the ingredients of the meal.

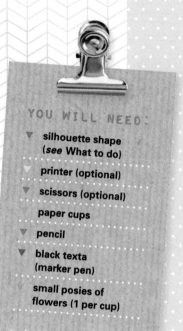

SILHOUETTE VASES

A silhouette is a striking and simple way to decorate a cup, and these 'vases' of flowers add a lovely final touch to your table. I suggest making two or three.

    If you aren't keen on drawing, you could print off the silhouette and stick it directly onto the cup instead; just ensure the edges are very neat. However, I would advise giving drawing a go – I find drawing silhouettes very relaxing and calming.

WHAT TO DO

1. Find a silhouette shape you like in the free clip-art section on your computer (or if you are artistic just draw your own). Print it off, cut it out and trace around it onto your paper cup with pencil. (You don't have to print it off if you feel confident with your drawing; just keep it on your screen as a guide.)

2. Go over the outline with black texta then colour in the silhouette in black.

3. Put a little water into each cup and add small posies of flowers.

PAPER-CROSS LIGHTS

Keep the paper theme going with some gently glowing lights. The cut-out paper cross in these jars allows some of the light to escape, and the glowing paper adds ambience.

WHAT TO DO

1. Wash the jars and dry them thoroughly.

2. Measure the circumference of the jars, adding 1 cm (½ in) extra to allow for an overlap for neatness. Next measure the height of each jar, either from the base to the top or, if the jar has a rim, to about 2 cm (¾ in) below the rim, i.e. so that the paper will sit nice and flat on the jar and not have to wrap around any curves. As an example, if your jar is 32 cm (12½ in) around the circumference and 9 cm (3½ in) from the base to the top, you need to cut out a piece of paper 33 cm x 9 cm (13 in x 3½ in) in size.

3. The crosses need to appear on opposite sides of the jar, so wrap the paper around the jar and mark the spots where the crosses need to be drawn before actually drawing them. Draw two fat cross shapes on each sheet of paper. The size of the crosses will depend on the size of your paper, but, as an example, my paper crosses were 5 cm x 5 cm (2 in x 2 in) overall, and the arms were all about 1.5 cm (½ in) wide.

4. Using a craft knife or scissors, carefully cut out the cross shapes, discarding the bits you cut out. Wrap the paper around the outside of the jars and secure it with either double-sided tape or craft glue. It's not vital to secure with tape or glue, as you'll tie the paper up with string; however, it makes the jars look much neater and keeps the paper in place.

5. Wrap rustic string a couple of times around the base of each jar, tying it in a neat knot.

6. Pop a tea light or two inside each jar.

7. If using battery-operated LED tea lights, you can spray-paint the lid and pop the lid on too. Don't do this if using real candles though.

YOU WILL NEED:

- old jars (jam, pickles, olives etc; lids optional)
- tape measure
- scissors
- sheets of paper (brown paper, newspaper, old book pages, maps, wrapping paper etc)
- pencil
- craft knife
- double-sided tape or craft glue
- rustic string
- tea lights (battery-operated or real candles)
- spray-paint (optional)

FLOWERS AND LIGHTS THEME

This is a pretty simple idea, but it looks absolutely gorgeous when the table is set. The long row of flowers and candles looks pretty, stylish and full of impact. Buy bunches of flowers that are in season to keep the cost down, and, if you have a garden, add leaves from your garden for the foliage.

TABLE CENTREPIECE

In the weeks leading up to your dinner party, keep any jars and bottles rather than recycling them, or go through your cupboards and see what you already have. The quantity you'll need will depend on the size of your table, but the effectiveness of this display lies in the sheer amount of jars and bottles that are arranged.

Whichever way you go about collecting the jars, clean them all thoroughly and remove any labels. Fill the jars with short bunches of flowers (so that your flowers don't obstruct guests sitting across the table from each other), then arrange them in a long row along the table. See the Styling with Jars chapter commencing on page 7 for ways to decorate you jars.

BANANA LEAF TEA LIGHTS

Cut strips of banana leaf about 13 cm (5 in) long and 2½ cm (1 in) high. Wrap the banana leaf strips around the metallic or plastic casing of LED tea lights and tie with rustic string to secure.

LACE WASHI-TAPE TEA LIGHTS

Find battery-operated LED tea lights in craft and discount shops. Stick lace washi tape or any other pretty washi tape (flowers work well) around the candles' metallic or plastic casing, then add the tea lights to your table display.

BANANA LEAF PLACE SETTINGS WITH FLAGS

For this project, try to find straws that tie in with the flowers on your table; green, hot pink or red straws often work well.

WHAT TO DO

1. Find a font on your computer you like and type the names of your guests into a document (one name per line with a couple of lines between each name, and indent the names about 8 cm/3 in in from the left-hand side of the page). Print the names out onto the piece of card.

2. Cut around the names to form rectangles about 14 cm x 2 cm (5½ in x ¾ in).

3. Fold each rectangle in half and glue the two sides of the card together around the top of each straw, ensuring the name appears clearly on one side of the flag.

4. Cut out a 'V' shape from the end of each rectangle to create a chevron shape in the flag.

5. Cut out squares of banana leaves and place a piece on top of each guest's dinner plate.

6. Put a flag on top of each place setting's banana leaf.

YOU WILL NEED:

- ▼ printer and piece of thin card
- ▼ scissors
- ▼ craft glue
- ▼ fun colourful straws (1 per flag)
- ▼ long lengths of banana leaf strips

KIDS' BIRTHDAY PARTIES

Kids' parties can be great fun, although I know they strike fear into many parents. With some pre-planning, parties can be both fun to organise and to host, and they don't need to cost a fortune. I find it actually helps, rather than hinders, if a child picks a theme, although I must admit the time my son requested (and got) a 'pirate, princess and octopus party', I found myself having to think and work quite a bit harder! Once the theme has been decided upon, it's then simply a matter of styling your party and your games around it.

PLANNING YOUR PARTY

Obviously you can go out and buy a multitude of things to suit your theme, and by all means do this if you like. However, if your theme is a little bit 'out there' or you want to make your party look different, here are some simple ways to bring your theme to life.

▼ Create bunting (*see* pp. 112–13 and pp. 118–19). If you're not a good sewer, you can use an iron-on no-sew hem product or glue.

▼ Think about how you're going to decorate the food table. If you have lots of themed plates, bowls and cups, you might want to keep the tablecloth a plain colour to let the crockery shine. Alternatively it's quite simple to make a tablecloth to match your theme. A cheap way to create a large tablecloth is to cut a flat sheet to the right size.

▼ If possible, I also theme the food, but keep it simple. I make flags to give a name to the food – the kids love to read what they are about to eat. This is easy with a theme like Star Wars or themes with lots of characters, as you just name all the food after a character!

▼ To theme your games just think of generic games, like Pin the Tail on the Donkey, and make them work for your theme – Pin the Light Sabre on Yoda, or Pin the Helmet on the Racing Driver's Head and so on. Once, when my son had lost both his front teeth just before his birthday, I drew a large set of teeth, printed a large photo of my son and played Pin the Teeth on the Six Year Old. His friends thought this was hilarious.

I find it's vital to draw up a plan for the party. This lists all the games we are going to play, what equipment I might need (such as balloons, a bat, any dress-ups) and, if there are going to be prizes, what these are. This helps to keep the party under control and flowing smoothly.

Despite giving a start time for parties, kids will often arrive in dribs and drabs. To keep the excitement levels from getting out of control, I start the games as soon as a few kids have arrived, but I always start with a game that people can gradually join as they arrive – a Pin the Tail on ... type of game is ideal for this.

*If we are going to play team games and there are quite
a few kids coming to the party, I plan the teams beforehand
with my child's input. This can help prevent petty arguments
and once again keeps the party running smoothly.*

*I always plan a few quiet games for just before eating
time. Games such as Simon Says, drawing games and even
Sleeping Kings and Queens (or Sleeping Ninjas, Sleeping
Pirates etc) are ideal to calm everyone down. While these
are happening, it gives you a chance to apply finishing
touches to the food.*

LOLLY BAGS/GOING HOME GIFT

In many cultures it is traditional to give a lolly
bag to the children as a going home gift. I
have always tried to find alternatives to just
lollies and cheap plastic toys. For example,
one year I bought each child a small watering
can and put a packet of seeds in it. Many
of the parents reported back that their kids
had planted the seeds and loved watching
them grow.

Another way to keep down the cost of
lolly bags is to use the prizes from games as
gifts. At the beginning of the party, I give each
child an empty lolly bag (or a takeaway noodle
box that I have customized to the theme;
see p. 47) with their name on it, which is
then put on the table or mantelpiece. Then as
games are held and prizes are won, I tell the
kids to put their prizes in their bags. For many
games I give everyone a small prize and I keep
an eye on who is winning to ensure prizes are
fairy distributed. Then at the end of the party
I might add a glittery pen and something else
small, and that's the lolly bag sorted.

BAKING PARTY THEME

A baking and decorating party is ideal for many ages and both girls and boys, and you can adjust it to suit the abilities of the kids coming to the party. We had a brilliant baking party for my son's second birthday. The kids had so much fun not only eating the cakes that they'd decorated, but also being allowed to go totally overboard with the sprinkles and other adornments!

This theme works well not only for birthday parties, but also for something to do during the holidays. Why not get the kids together before Christmas to bake and decorate Christmas cookies to give to family and friends or to hang on the tree?

For younger ones, the decorating is often the most fun part, as they can get bored very quickly with the mixing and baking. So if the party is for younger children I prepare a whole lot of cupcakes and biscuits in advance ready for decorating.

Older kids often like to get more involved with the actual baking. In this case have the biscuit dough already made and then get the kids to roll it out and cut out their shapes. While the biscuits are cooking and cooling, have a few games ready to play.

You can, of course, get the kids to do everything – the mixing, the cutting out and the baking. This works best with a smaller group of kids.

See p. 179 for cupcake and biscuit recipes for this theme.

ICING OPTIONS

I make two different types of icing that the children can use to decorate with. The cream cheese and jam icing is great for cupcakes, because sprinkles and other decorations stick well to it and most kids like this style of icing. I also make a simple water icing. You could make the butter icing from Worm and Maggot Cupcakes on p. 137 too, omitting the cocoa powder and adding an extra 2 tablespoons of icing sugar.

CREAM CHEESE AND JAM ICING

Covers about 12 cupcakes

WHAT TO DO

1. Put the cream cheese in a bowl and whisk with a fork until loosened and smooth.

2. Add the sieved strawberry jam and mix well.

3. Store in the fridge until needed.

BASIC WATER ICING

Covers about 16 biscuits

WHAT TO DO

1. Sift the icing sugar into a bowl then slowly add about 1 tablespoon of cold water, stirring the mixture until you have a smooth, but not too runny, icing.

2. If you want to colour the icing, add a drop or two of your chosen colour(s). I tend not to colour the icing as it usually gets covered in vast amounts of sprinkles and other decorations!

3. Set aside until needed, then give it a stir when ready to use.

YOU WILL NEED:

- 250 g (9 oz) cream cheese
- 3 tablespoons strawberry jam, sieved

YOU WILL NEED:

- 120 g (4½ oz) icing (confectioners') sugar
- food colouring (optional)

CAKE DECORATIONS

Have all your cupcake and biscuit decorations ready to go, dispensed into small bowls. There are simply hundreds of different sprinkles, sparkles, candy shapes and toppers to choose from. I also have plenty of icing pens ready to go – these are great for adding detail. You can get icing pens from supermarkets, speciality cake shops and many craft shops. They come ready-filled with icing and have a very fine tip – you just snip off the end and they're ready to write or draw with.

When you're ready to go, gather the children around and get them to ice their cupcake/cookie first, then let them go crazy with the decorating!

Yes, you will find that half the kids only eat the icing and decorations and the other half eat only their cake! And if you have the party in the garden (which is always a good idea because of the mess), you will find half-eaten cupcakes and biscuits for weeks to come! But encouraging kids to cook from a young age and letting them take charge is a great way to foster a passion for cooking.

FUN WITH STYLING

You can keep the 'sprinkle' theme going by looking for spotty accessories (one of my favourite styles), such as spotty napkins, bowls, plates and straws. If you're going to bake the cupcakes or cookies during the party, while they are cooking, give the kids white paper cups and/or plain-coloured plates and lots of spotty stickers and get them to decorate the cups/plates for a fun activity to pass the time. (If using plates, ask the kids to stick to the rims or you may end up with spots stuck to the roof of the kids' mouths!)

You could also decorate the tops of white balloons with spotty stickers to look like sprinkles.

RACING PARTY THEME

This theme is all about chequers! The start and finish lines of a racetrack are instantly recognisable, as is the chequered flag, so use this idea to theme as much or as little of your party as you like.

CHEQUERED-FLAG BUNTING

If you have a sewing machine you may choose to sew these; however, I find it quicker to glue them together. Fabric widths vary, so the amount of flags you'll make from each strip will vary, but each strip should make about six flags.

WHAT TO DO

1. Take the material and fold over a 20 cm (8 in) strip from the end of the material. Cut along this length, i.e. where the two bits of material meet, not along the fold (so you will end up with a piece that's 40 cm/16 in long and whatever the width of your fabric is).

2. Keep the material folded in half and mark the top (the folded edge) and bottom every 16 cm (6 in) with chalk. Cut through the material at the marks, so you'll end up with several folded rectangles, each 16 cm x 20 cm (6 in x 8 in), with the exception of the one at the end (unless your fabric width is exactly divisible by 16!). The material I used yielded six rectangles.

3. Keeping the rectangles folded, mark the middle of each rectangle on the shorter side (i.e. at the 8 cm/3 in point) where the two bits of material meet, not on the folded edge. Draw lines from this centre point up to each corner, to create triangles. Cut out the triangles.

4. Repeat steps 1 to 3 to make a second lot of bunting. Once again, the width of your fabric will determine how many you can make each time.

5. Glue (or sew if you prefer) the edges of the triangles together, leaving 1–2 cm (½–1 in) towards the top fold unglued.

6. Tie the ribbon onto a metal skewer and use this to thread the ribbon through the top ends of the flags. Iron the flags.

7. Using sticky tape or pins, hang the bunting in front of a table, in a doorway or on a wall, spreading the flags out so that they're evenly spaced.

YOU WILL NEED:

- about 90 cm (36 in) black-and-white chequered material (this should make about 12 flags with a bit of material left over, although the final number will depend on the width of your material)

- scissors

- chalk

- craft glue suitable for fabric (or sewing machine)

- at least 300 cm (10 ft) black ribbon

- metal skewer

- iron and ironing board

- sticky tape (Scotch tape) or pins

RACETRACK BIRTHDAY CAKE

This birthday cake can be adapted to whatever age your child is. The number '8' makes a particularly nice racetrack!

You will need to use either a square or rectangular cake and the size will depend on how many people you want to feed. Bake (or buy) your child's favourite cake and then follow the icing instructions below. The size of your cake will determine how much butter icing you'll need, but an average sized square birthday cake will need about two quantities of icing.

For the different butter icings used, follow the recipe in Worm and Maggot Cupcakes on p. 137 (which is one full quantity), omitting the cocoa powder and adding an extra 2 tablespoons of icing sugar.

An icing pen is used for the white 'road markings'; you can get icing pens from supermarkets, speciality cake shops and many craft shops. They come ready-filled with icing and have a very fine tip – you just snip off the end and they're ready to go.

WHAT TO DO

1. Once the cake has cooled, use the toothpick to prick out the outline of the number on top of the cake. (The number is whatever age the child is.) The outline should be wide enough to create a nice racetrack.

2. Fill the inside of the number with black icing (the road), smoothing the icing with a warm blunt knife.

3. Next pipe red icing around the edge of the number.

4. Cover the remainder of the top of the cake with green icing (to represent grass). You could just spread it on with a knife, but I find it easier to pipe it, particularly if you have to fill the inside of a number.

5. Using the white icing pen, pipe white lines along the middle of the number to represent road markings.

6. Ice the sides of the cake with the white butter icing.

7. Use your printer to make a little 'Happy Birthday' banner. Use the 'Insert/ Table' function in Word and, using the photo as a guide, fill in every other square black. Leave the middle squares empty and write your birthday message there. Print off the chequered flag and cut it out. Fold over the two ends and secure them onto two wooden skewers with either glue or sticky tape. Stick the banner into the cake.

8. Cover the cake board with the chequered material, securing it under the board with either glue or tape, then sit the decorated cake on it.

9. Place a small toy car on the track and add the candles.

RACING FLAGS FOR THE TABLE

These flags add a fabulous pop of racy-red colour to the table.

Makes 4 flags

WHAT TO DO

1. Cut out four rectangles of fabric each about 18 cm x 12 cm (7 in x 5 in).

2. Working on one rectangle at a time, fold over a 1 cm (½ in) border on each side and stick the borders down with glue.

3. Iron the rectangles (flags).

4. Working on one flag at a time, put the flag in front of you on a table with the hems facing upwards and so the long sides are parallel to the edge of the table. Fold over about 2.5 cm (1 in) of fabric on one of the short sides. Put a chopstick in the fold, stopping just short of the top of the material, then glue the flap down so the chopstick stays in place.

5. Arrange the flags in a glass on the table.

RACING-CAR BISCUITS

Bake a whole lot of racing car–shaped biscuits before the big day (*see* recipe p. 179) and get the kids to decorate their own cars. The easiest way to do this is to buy several different coloured icing pens from the supermarket baking section and let the kids go crazy with their own designs. You may like to make a few in advance (like the ones in the photo) that the kids can copy; you could include some with the age of the child as the car's number. But it's really more about letting the kids use their own imagination. You could also make a basic water icing (*see* p. 109) and buy some sprinkles for the kids to decorate their biscuits with.

IDEAS FOR GAMES

You could do a different take on Pin the Tail on the Donkey, e.g. Pin the Racing-Car Driver in the Car or Pin the Helmet on the Racing Driver's Head.

Another fun game is racing with cardboard-box cars. You'll need one car for each team. Cut three-quarters of the bottom out of old cardboard boxes for legs to go through (the remaining quarter becomes the 'bonnet' of the car, i.e. you turn the box upside-down before you climb in). Cover the sides of each box in coloured paper (taping or gluing it onto the box), depending on your team colours.

Turn the box upside down, so the 'bonnet' is on the top. Paint or draw the front, back and sides of a racing car onto each one; for example, add stripes, wheels and wheel arches, a team number and a team name. If you have braces you could attach pairs to the front and back of the boxes to hook over the drivers' shoulders, but this isn't vital; the kids can always just hold the boxes up with their hands while they race.

Split the kids into teams and place a 'starting line' on the floor. The starting line can either be the one you made for your front door (if you made one; *see* ideas below) or simply some black squares drawn onto a long piece of paper in a chequered pattern. Easier still, just have an imaginary starting line! Send each team's first driver off on a lap. When they've completed a lap, get them out of the racing car quickly and pass it on to the next child. Repeat until all the kids have had a turn. You could also add a helmet into the mix for each team and, of course, you'll need a flag to signal the winning team crossing the line.

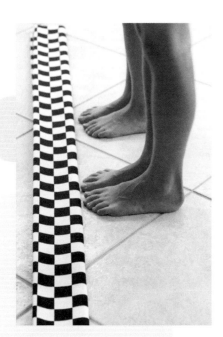

OTHER IDEAS FOR THE RACING PARTY THEME:

▼ Create a 'starting line' for guests to cross over when they enter the party. Do this by simply laying down a piece of chequered fabric about 100 cm x 20 cm (40 in x 8 in) near the front door.

▼ Use black-and-white chequered material to make a tablecloth. Hem it with no-sew hemming tape (*see* p. 72 for how to use this tape).

▼ Have lots of black and white balloons.

▼ Either buy black-and-white chequered paper or print it off, then cut it into strips to glue around paper drinking cups. If you can find tape that looks like a road in craft or party shops, you could also stick lengths of this around the cups. Finish with black-and-white striped straws.

SUPERHERO PARTY THEME

I don't think I've ever come across a child – girl or boy – who doesn't want to have super powers. And let's not forget the outfit: who can resist a cape?

If your child has a specific superhero in mind for this party theme, create your styling and games around this character. Alternatively mix and match your superheroes.

SUPERHERO BUNTING

This bunting will knock the kids' socks off – kapow!

If you have a sewing machine you may choose to sew these; however, it's just as quick to glue them together. Fabric widths vary, so the amount of flags you'll make from each strip will vary, but each strip should make about six flags.

WHAT TO DO

1. Take the superhero fabric and fold over a 20 cm (8 in) strip from the end of the material. Cut along this length, i.e. where the two bits of material meet, not along the fold (so you will end up with a piece that's 40 cm/16 in long and whatever the width of your fabric is).

2. Keep the material folded in half and mark the top (the folded edge) and bottom every 16 cm (6 in) with chalk. Cut through the material at the marks, so you'll end up with several folded rectangles, each 16 cm x 20 cm (6 in x 8 in), with the exception of the one at the end (unless your fabric width is exactly divisible by 16!). The material I used yielded six rectangles.

3. Keeping the rectangles folded, mark the middle of each rectangle on the shorter side (i.e. at the 8 cm/3 in point) where the two bits of material meet, not on the folded edge. Draw lines from this centre point up to each corner, to create triangles. Cut out the triangles.

4. Repeat steps 1 to 3 to make a second lot of bunting. Once again, the width of your fabric will determine how many you can make each time.

5. Glue (or sew if you prefer) the edges of the triangles together, leaving 1–2 cm (½–1 in) towards the top fold unglued.

6. Tie the coloured ribbon onto a metal skewer and use this to thread the ribbon through the top ends of the flags. Iron the flags.

7. Using sticky tape or pins, hang the bunting in front of a table, in a doorway or on a wall, spreading the flags out so that they're evenly spaced.

YOU WILL NEED:

- about 90 cm (36 in) superhero fabric (this should make about 12 flags with a bit of material left over, although the final number will depend on the width of your material)
- scissors
- chalk
- craft glue suitable for fabric (or sewing machine)
- at least 300 cm (10 ft) ribbon
- metal skewer
- iron and ironing board
- sticky tape (Scotch tape) or pins

SUPERHERO CUPCAKE TOPPERS

These are a really simple but effective way to enhance the superhero theme. Another way to approach this project is to make blank speech bubbles as opposed to ones with messages already written on them. Do this by sticking blank speech-bubble stickers onto card and cutting them out. Stick a toothpick onto the back of each speech bubble and get the kids to write their own words in the bubbles.

WHAT TO DO

1. Cut out superhero pictures and speech bubbles from comics or wrapping paper and glue them onto the card, or print your own designs onto the card.

2. Cut each picture and speech bubble out.

3. Put each picture image-side down then place a toothpick or wooden skewer on top of each one, ensuring that the toothpick doesn't go above the top of the picture and extends beneath the bottom of it.

4. Stick each toothpick to the back of each picture with a small piece of sticky tape.

5. Add a topper to each cupcake.

SUPERHERO SPEECH BUBBLES

Either draw or print some superhero speech bubbles, like the ones below, with words like 'Bam!' and 'Kapow!' written on them. Stick them onto some thin card, cut them out and then Blu Tack them up around the house.

YOU WILL NEED:

▼ scissors
▼ superhero comics or wrapping paper or your own designed speech bubbles
▼ craft glue
▼ thin white card
▼ toothpicks or wooden skewers
▼ sticky tape (Scotch tape)

- a long roll of white paper or butcher's paper, just a bit longer than the tallest child attending the party and at least 46 cm (18 in) wide (available at shops like Ikea)

- thick black texta (marker pen)

- scissors

- pencil

- 3–4 pieces of A3 paper or extra paper from the long roll

- blue single sheet or large piece of blue fabric (white would work too if that's easier – just pretend it's an overcast day!)

- sticky tape (Scotch tape)

- props such as capes, masks etc (optional)

- ladder

- camera

- printer (optional)

SUPERHERO PHOTO BOOTH

This is a lot of fun and provides party memories for all the kids. Essentially you are creating a city skyline (maybe even Gotham City) that the kids lie down on and pretend to fly across. Photos of the kids are taken from above so they look like they are flying through the sky.

WHAT TO DO

1. Roll out the paper and, using the black texta, draw a city skyline on it. If you aren't sure what to draw, there are plenty of images on the internet you can use as reference, or copy what's drawn in the photo opposite. You only need to draw the outlines of the buildings; there's no need to colour them in.

2. Cut roughly around the outline of the city skyline.

3. Draw and cut out a few cloud shapes from the extra paper.

4. Lay the blue sheet/material out on the floor. Stick the skyline across the bottom of it and the clouds up above. Get the kids to lie on the city scene one by one doing their best flying superhero impressions. You might like to have a few props on hand such as capes and masks.

5. Using a ladder (or any high vantage point), take a photo of each child in action. If you have a printer at home, print the photos straight away. Alternatively email them to the kids afterwards as a thank you for coming to the party.

PIN THE CAPE ON THE SUPERHERO

Using either a large piece of butcher's paper or an A3 sheet of cardboard, draw and colour in the back of a superhero (a superhero is, of course, usually identified by wearing their underpants on the outside of their outfit). Stick this to a wall using Blu Tack. Draw a cape on a separate piece of card in proportion to your superhero picture, stick Blu Tack to the top of it and then you're ready to start the game.

Remember to agree beforehand where you think the correct position for the cape should be! Using a scarf, blindfold each child one at a time and spin them around a couple of times. Hand them the cape and ask them to position it on the picture where they think it should go. I usually guide them a bit by letting them feel the edges of the picture. Write their first initial on the picture at the spot where they stuck the top of the cape and then continue with the remaining kids. The winner is the child whose initial is closest to the agreed spot.

SUPERHERO CREATION GAME

Our family has an absolutely favourite superhero game that we play not only at parties, but also on long car journeys, on train journeys and while waiting in queues. This one's not just for kids!

Each person has to think of three things: their superhero name; their superhero costume; and their two superhero powers.

Give everyone 4–5 minutes of thinking time, then, one by one, let the kids tell everyone about their superhero (cape or no cape is always a hot topic). For example, my child's superhero name is Electrode. His super power is that he can shoot electricity from his fingers and hold lightning bolts. His costume is black with a silver lightning bolt on the chest and it most definitely doesn't have a cape.

Depending on the age of the kids, you could also give them paper and pencils to draw their superhero costume.

EASTER

Easter is usually thought of as a time of renewal, as in many countries it is spring, which means blossoming flowers and baby animals being born. It's the opposite in the Southern Hemisphere, of course, where Easter falls in autumn and the leaves start falling from the trees. Whichever season you are in, it's fun to decorate your Easter table in pretty pastels or vibrant colours, or make a stunning log table (see p. 132) that you can use all year round.

This can be used as a table centrepiece to make a statement: 'It's Easter! Come celebrate with us!'

WHAT TO DO

1. Using the pin or scalpel, carefully prick a hole in the top and bottom of each egg. Make the hole in the bottom a little bit bigger than the one in the top, about 3–4 mm (⅛ in) in diameter. Push a wooden skewer into the bigger hole, using it to gently break up the egg yolk. Remove the skewer. Holding the egg over a bowl, blow into the smaller of the two holes until the yolk and egg white comes out of the bottom of the egg into the bowl (save these for scrambled eggs or omelettes!). You'll probably find it takes a blow or two to get it going. Repeat until all of the eggs have had their contents removed. Gently rinse the eggs and leave to dry.

2. If dyeing the eggs, make up the egg dyes according to the packet instructions and dye them. If you'd rather use paint, use the paintbrush to paint the eggs in your desired colour/pattern. You will probably need to do two or three coats.

3. To be able to hang the eggs, straighten out the paperclip, but leave one end still bent in a hook shape. Take a 30 cm (12 in) piece of thread and thread it through two holes on a button. Slide the button along until it is halfway along the thread. Tie a loose knot in the thread. Hook the knotted end onto the paperclip and insert it into the larger hole in the egg and then out through the top, so the button is covering the bottom hole. Untie the knot and thread each end of thread through two holes in another button. Slide it down until it sits on top of the egg. Retie the knot.

4. Strip off any leaves from the branch and put it in the vase. If you're using a vase that's not see-through and you find that the branch won't stand up properly, stick a ball of Blu Tack in the bottom and stick the branch into this.

5. Hang the decorated eggs onto the branch so that they hang at different heights.

- a pin or scalpel
- about 12 eggs
- wooden skewer
- egg dye or paints suitable to paint eggshells in the colours of your choice
- 125 ml (4 fl oz) white vinegar (optional, may be required for egg dye; check packet instructions)
- paintbrush (if painting rather than dyeing)
- paperclip
- invisible or coloured thread
- buttons (2 for each egg)
- 1 long dead branch with several smaller branches coming off it
- tall vase with a narrow neck
- Blu Tack (optional)

IDEAS FOR HOW TO DECORATE YOUR EGGS:

- Keep it very simple and just dye them in three different colours.

- Using crayons, spell out the words 'Happy Easter' over 11 eggs, i.e. one letter per egg.

- Paint with swirls and dots.

- Leave the eggs undyed and unpainted and use a black texta (marker pen) to draw bunny silhouettes (you can find in the free clip-art on your computer) on the eggs.

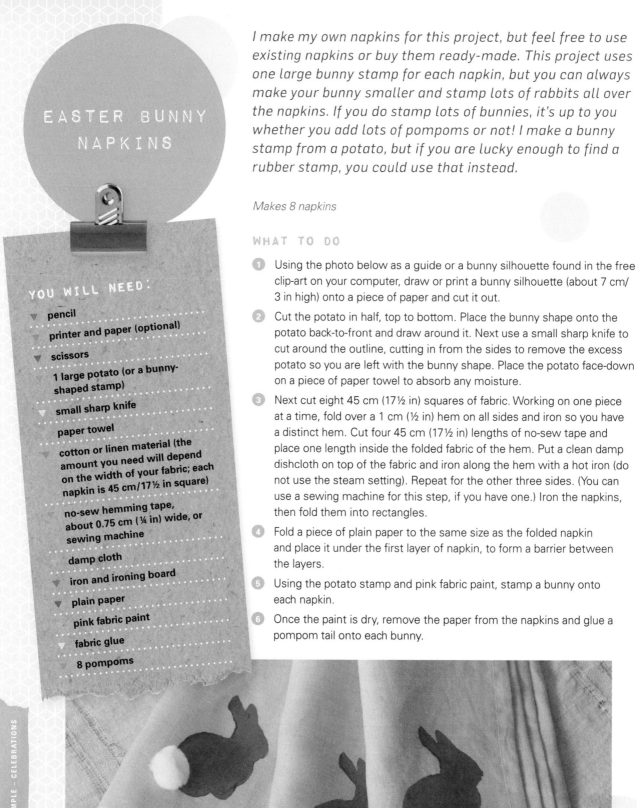

EASTER BUNNY NAPKINS

I make my own napkins for this project, but feel free to use existing napkins or buy them ready-made. This project uses one large bunny stamp for each napkin, but you can always make your bunny smaller and stamp lots of rabbits all over the napkins. If you do stamp lots of bunnies, it's up to you whether you add lots of pompoms or not! I make a bunny stamp from a potato, but if you are lucky enough to find a rubber stamp, you could use that instead.

Makes 8 napkins

WHAT TO DO

1 Using the photo below as a guide or a bunny silhouette found in the free clip-art on your computer, draw or print a bunny silhouette (about 7 cm/ 3 in high) onto a piece of paper and cut it out.

2 Cut the potato in half, top to bottom. Place the bunny shape onto the potato back-to-front and draw around it. Next use a small sharp knife to cut around the outline, cutting in from the sides to remove the excess potato so you are left with the bunny shape. Place the potato face-down on a piece of paper towel to absorb any moisture.

3 Next cut eight 45 cm (17½ in) squares of fabric. Working on one piece at a time, fold over a 1 cm (½ in) hem on all sides and iron so you have a distinct hem. Cut four 45 cm (17½ in) lengths of no-sew tape and place one length inside the folded fabric of the hem. Put a clean damp dishcloth on top of the fabric and iron along the hem with a hot iron (do not use the steam setting). Repeat for the other three sides. (You can use a sewing machine for this step, if you have one.) Iron the napkins, then fold them into rectangles.

4 Fold a piece of plain paper to the same size as the folded napkin and place it under the first layer of napkin, to form a barrier between the layers.

5 Using the potato stamp and pink fabric paint, stamp a bunny onto each napkin.

6 Once the paint is dry, remove the paper from the napkins and glue a pompom tail onto each bunny.

YOU WILL NEED:

- pencil
- printer and paper (optional)
- scissors
- 1 large potato (or a bunny-shaped stamp)
- small sharp knife
- paper towel
- cotton or linen material (the amount you need will depend on the width of your fabric; each napkin is 45 cm/17½ in square)
- no-sew hemming tape, about 0.75 cm (¼ in) wide, or sewing machine
- damp cloth
- iron and ironing board
- plain paper
- pink fabric paint
- fabric glue
- 8 pompoms

BEAUTIFUL JARS OF EASTER TREATS

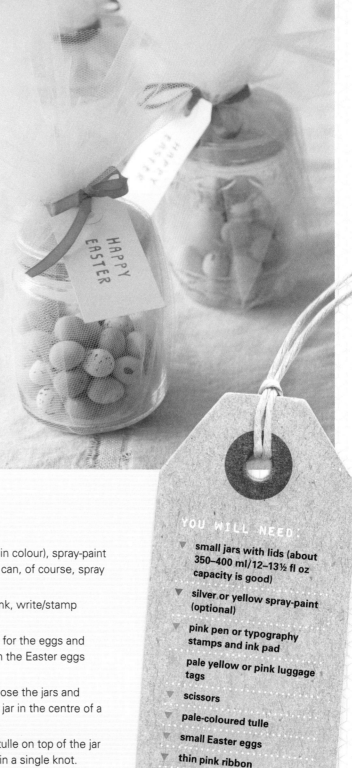

These not only look beautiful on your Easter table, but make gorgeous Easter gifts too.

WHAT TO DO

1. If using jars with patterned lids (as opposed to a plain colour), spray-paint the lids silver or yellow, then leave them to dry. You can, of course, spray your lids even if they aren't patterned.

2. Using either a pink pen or typography stamps and ink, write/stamp 'Happy Easter' on the luggage tags.

3. Scrunch up a small piece of tulle to use as the base for the eggs and place in the bottom of each jar. Then fill the jars with the Easter eggs and put the lids on.

4. Cut up more tulle into squares large enough to enclose the jars and have about an extra 10 cm (4 in) at the top. Sit each jar in the centre of a tulle piece.

5. Cut pieces of ribbon 50 cm (20 in) long. Bunch the tulle on top of the jar and wrap the ribbon twice around the tulle, tying it in a single knot.

6. Thread the ribbon through the luggage tag hole, then tie the ribbon in a bow. To get a bow that looks elegant and sits flat, tie the knot as normal and form the first loop. For the second loop, go behind the first loop instead of in front (which is more usual) and then form the second loop. Gently tighten the bow.

YOU WILL NEED:

- small jars with lids (about 350–400 ml/12–13½ fl oz capacity is good)
- silver or yellow spray-paint (optional)
- pink pen or typography stamps and ink pad
- pale yellow or pink luggage tags
- scissors
- pale-coloured tulle
- small Easter eggs
- thin pink ribbon

NESTING PLATES

YOU WILL NEED:

- ▼ crockery
- ▼ scissors
- ▼ pink or yellow ribbon
- ▼ green-coloured straw (available from craft shops, especially around Easter)
- ▼ Easter eggs (3 per nest)

An easy way to pretty up your table is to wrap each place setting in pink or yellow ribbon, finishing with a bow and a 'nest'.

WHAT TO DO

1. Choose your crockery – matching or otherwise. It really doesn't matter these days if you have a perfect set, but try and find at least one large and one small plate (or small bowl) for each setting. Stack the plates on top of each other at each setting.

2. Cut lengths of ribbon that are long enough to tie once around the top plate at each place setting with some left over for a bow.

3. For each place setting, put the ribbon under the middle of the top plate then bring it up over the top, finishing with a bow off to one side of the plate. To get a bow that looks elegant and sits flat, tie the knot as normal and form the first loop. For the second loop, go behind the first loop instead of in front (which is more usual) and then form the second loop. Gently tighten the bow.

4. Separate the green straw into portions that are big enough to form a 'nest' for each plate. Using your hands, shape the straw into round nests.

5. Put a nest on each top plate, slipping the bottom of each one just under the ribbon.

6. Add three Easter eggs to each nest.

FUZZY EASTER NESTS

I came up with this idea when I was trying to work out how to form wool nests that wouldn't lose their shape. I wrapped some wool around a small bowl to get the desired shape, and then realised it was far simpler to keep the dish in place to hold the structure together, rather than working out a complicated way!

WHAT TO DO

1. Measure the depth of your bowl on the outside from the base to the top and cut six lengths of double-sided tape this size. Stick the tape (vertically) on the outside of the bowl at equal distances around the bowl.

2. Next stick a length of tape around the base of the bowl and another one around the circumference at the top, both on the outside.

3. Take the end of the wool and stick it to the tape at the base, then wind it around the rest of the base. Keep wrapping the wool around and around going up the bowl, sticking it to the tape as you go and keeping the layers neat and even. Once you get to the top, cut the wool and stick the end securely to the tape. Carefully fluff the wool a little to make it look more like a nest.

4. Fill the bowl with Easter eggs.

5. Repeat steps 1–4 for as many nests as you'd like to make.

YOU WILL NEED:

▼ ruler
▼ shallow dishes, preferably delicate ones
▼ scissors
▼ double-sided tape
▼ bright-coloured wool
▼ Easter eggs

TREE-STUMP EGG NEST

YOU WILL NEED

YOU WILL NEED

- a tree stump
- sandpaper
- 7–8 cm (3–3½ in) paintbrush
- white house paint
- pink paint
- bowl of Easter eggs and fluffy chicks

Okay, so not everyone has a tree stump lying around, but once you start looking you might be lucky enough to find one. I found one through a friend who'd had to chop down a tree, and another when someone had inconsiderately (and illegally) dumped a chopped-up tree down the road from us. This tree-stump nest doubles as a great log table or stool outside of Easter.

WHAT TO DO

1. I find it is easier and cleaner to paint the stump if the bark has been removed, so strip off the bark and sand down any rough bits.
2. Paint the bottom half of the trunk with the white paint, diluting the paint slightly if you would like a more rustic look.
3. Allow the paint to dry before painting a pink stripe around the middle of the stump.
4. Once the stump is completely dry, move it into place at your front door and sit a pretty bowl of Easter eggs and fluffy chicks on top.

EASTER PICNIC SET

If the weather is fine, why not go on an Easter picnic?

WHAT TO DO

1. Stick lengths of washi tape onto the top and bottom of the paper bags.
2. Paint a rabbit silhouette in between the washi tape strips, using the picture above as a guide, or find a bunny silhouette in the free clip-art on your computer.
3. Wrap washi tape strips around the bottom of each cutlery piece. Place one set of cutlery into each bag, with a paper napkin, a straw and a chocolate bunny.

YOU WILL NEED:

- washi tape
- brown paper bags (1 for each guest)
- pink and yellow paint
- paintbrush
- bamboo cutlery
- paper napkins
- fun straws
- foil-wrapped chocolate bunnies (1 for each guest)

HALLOWEEN

Halloween is becoming more and more popular around the world, not just in the States, and is enjoyed by kids and adults alike. Although a carved pumpkin is a great start to your Halloween display, there are lots of other fun and spooky ways to decorate your house and garden.

SCARY CUPCAKES

TOMBSTONE AND GHOST CUPCAKES

These cupcakes are simple and fun to make. You can pick up ready-made fondant icing and icing pens from supermarkets, speciality cake shops and many craft shops. These icing pens come filled with icing and have a very fine tip – you just snip off the end and they're ready to write or draw with.

I've provided a cupcake recipe in this book, but you could use a packet mix if you prefer! I have suggested using black fondant and a white pen, but you could just as easily reverse this.

Makes 12 cupcakes

WHAT TO DO

1. To start decorating the cupcakes, thinly roll out the black fondant icing with a rolling pin and, using the cookie cutter, stamp out 12 circles of icing.
2. Heat the jam briefly to melt it and then brush the tops of the cupcakes with it.
3. Stick the circles of icing onto the top of each cupcake, securing the circles with the jam.
4. Using the white icing pen, draw tombstones, ghosts and crosses on each icing circle, using the above photo as a guide.
5. Use the icing pens to add details such as 'RIP' to the tombstones and crosses.

YOU WILL NEED:

- 12 chocolate cupcakes (*see* recipe p. 179), cooled
- black fondant icing
- round cookie cutter (7 cm/2¾ in diameter, or diameter of cupcake tops)
- 2 tablespoons jam
- white icing pen
- black icing pen

WORM AND MAGGOT CUPCAKES

Kids love these – is there a better combination than a cupcake and a jelly snake? Not to mention the white and yellow 'maggot' sprinkles!

Makes 12 cupcakes

WHAT TO DO

1. Using electric beaters, beat the butter briefly.
2. Gradually add the icing sugar to the butter, sifting it in three separate batches and beating it into the butter after each addition.
3. Next sift the cocoa powder into the butter and whisk to combine. If the icing is too thick, whisk in some milk.
4. Use this chocolate icing to ice the cupcakes, leaving it rough rather than smoothing it out.
5. Using the pointy end of a sharp knife, make four small holes in the icing of each cupcake, going about 1 cm (½ in) into the cake part of each cupcake too.
6. Stick a jelly snake head or tail into each hole (you get to eat the middle bits!).
7. Add the 'maggots' by topping each cupcake with white and yellow sprinkles.

YOU WILL NEED:

- 12 chocolate cupcakes (*see* recipe p. 179), cooled
- 60 g (2 oz) butter, softened
- 150 g (5½ oz) icing (confectioner's) sugar
- 2 tablespoons cocoa powder, sifted
- 1–2 tablespoons milk (optional)
- 24 jelly snakes, each cut into 3 pieces
- white sprinkles
- yellow sprinkles

SIMPLE MUMMY LIGHTS

Make several of these and sit them on your mantelpiece or front path, or add a hanging loop to them and hang them from a tree. Alternatively, if you don't want to use them as lights, they're also great for holding straws or lollies (minus the tea light, of course). The size of your mummies will depend on the size of the jars; use old jam jars or, for larger mummies, coffee jars.

WHAT TO DO

1. First, decide whether you want to hang the lights up or not. If so, you need to make a hanging loop around the top of the jars before you add the mummy bandages. To work out the length of string you'll need to make a hanging loop, wrap a piece of string twice around the jar then make a loop roughly the length you want. Undo and measure the length you have used, adding on 5 cm (2 in) to make tying the knots easier. Make as many lengths as you need.

2. To make the hanging loop, take the measured string and wrap it twice around the top of the jar (in the groove), tying it in a loose single knot once you've gone around twice. Next take the long end of the string over the top of the jar to the opposite side and tuck it under both layers of string – this is why the first knot needs to be loose, otherwise it's too hard to tuck the string under. Pull the string until you have the desired loop length and tie a tight knot. Re-tie the loose knot to make it tight too. Cut off any excess string. Note that if you aren't hanging the jars from hooks, you may want to leave tying the second knot until you have looped the string over the tree branch.

3. Wrap each jar in your choice of bandage material and secure with double-sided tape. Alternatively simply tuck the ends securely under other layers of bandages.

4. Next, either stick on googly eyes, or draw eyes on the bandage material using the black texta.

5. Add an LED tea light to each jar (much safer than the real ones) then place the mummy lights on your mantelpiece, doorstep, front porch or wherever else you fancy. If hanging them up, hang on hooks or in trees.

6. Wait until it gets dark then turn on the tea lights to make your mummies come alive!

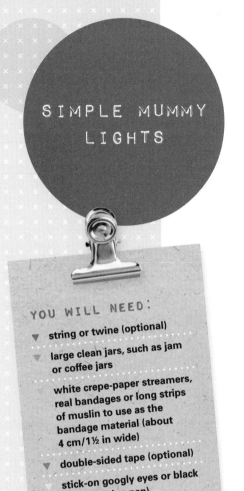

YOU WILL NEED:

- string or twine (optional)
- large clean jars, such as jam or coffee jars
- white crepe-paper streamers, real bandages or long strips of muslin to use as the bandage material (about 4 cm/1½ in wide)
- double-sided tape (optional)
- stick-on googly eyes or black texta (marker pen)
- LED tea lights

SPOOKY UPSIDE-DOWN GHOSTS

Make several of these spooky ghosts and hang them all around your house and garden, then watch your guests freak out!

WHAT TO DO

1. Lay the muslin flat on the ground. Using the above photo as a guide, draw the outline of a ghost onto the muslin with the texta, using the full length of the muslin.

2. Cut the ghost out, ensuring you cut inside the drawn outline so that you can't see any texta on the muslin.

3. Lay the ghost's 'head' on a piece of newspaper and paint eyes and a mouth onto the muslin. Alternatively simply cut the eyes and mouth out.

4. Attach the bottom of the ghost to the top of a doorway or to a tree with drawing-pins, so that it's hanging upside-down.

YOU WILL NEED:

- piece of sheer muslin about 130 cm (51 in) long (1 piece for each ghost)
- texta (marker pen)
- scissors
- newspaper
- paintbrush
- black paint
- drawing-pins (push pins/ thumbtacks)

HALLOWEEN WREATH

To make this wreath you need to ensure your branches are bendy enough, otherwise they'll just snap when you try to bend them into shape. Don't use dead branches, and if the branches still have leaves on them, strip them off before using. This project makes a wreath that's about 38 cm (15 in) in diameter, but the size of yours will depend on the length of the branches you use.

Some of the best places to find Halloween objects are local discount, craft and party shops.

YOU WILL NEED:

▼ 20–25 branches that are a bit bendy, or any foliage that bends; each branch should be about 50 cm (20 in) long

▼ florist's wire

▼ black netting, cobwebbing or muslin

▼ Halloween objects, such as skeletons, spiders, skulls, bones, bats and witches hats

▼ black twine or wide black ribbon

WHAT TO DO

1 To form the branches into a wreath shape, firstly take three of the branches and tie them together with the florist's wire. Do this by lining the branches up roughly side by side then twist a piece of wire several times around each end, about 2 cm (¾ in) from the ends. Repeat this step two more times to make three sets of branches.

2 Now tie the three sets together so they're ready to form a circle. To do this, take two sets and sit them almost end-to-end, but so they overlap by about 2–3 cm (¾–1¼ in). Tie the two ends securely together with more wire – they must be very secure, otherwise they'll just spring open when you try to form the circle.

3 Tie the third set of branches to one of the ends, as in step 2 (so you'll end up with one very long set of branches).

4 Form the branches into a circle, once again overlapping the ends that meet. Secure tightly with wire.

5 Use the remaining branches to fill out the wreath until you're happy with it. Do this by wrapping them around the branch circle, in and out in a spiral motion. Secure each branch with more wire, or simply tuck the ends in so they stay in place. Remember, this is a Halloween wreath so it doesn't have to be perfect!

6 To decorate the wreath, drape and wrap the netting you are using around the wreath in a loose fashion, allowing some to hang down.

7 Attach your chosen Halloween objects to the wreath by tucking some of the smaller things in between the branches, sitting things in the netting and propping things on the bottom inner circle and top of the wreath. (If you want to make the objects more secure, you could tie black twine around some of them and sew them into the netting, but I prefer to keep mine simple.)

8 To hang the wreath, double up the twine or ribbon and put the loop end around the top of the wreath. Stick the other (loose) ends of the twine through the loop and pull gently to secure. Tie the two loose ends together and hang the wreath on your front door or gate.

TRICK-OR-TREAT LOLLY-JAR DISPLAY

See if you can find a scary-looking font on your computer for the little signs that stick in these jars. If you have a colour printer, you could also sit the text in orange boxes and print these out. You can also simply hand-write the signs.

WHAT TO DO

1. Fill the jars with your selection of Halloween lollies.

2. Decide what icky things you want to write on the signs for the four jars. Things like 'Witches' Treats' or 'Rotten Bones' usually go down very well with the kids!

3. Find a scary-looking font on your computer, then write your messages using this font and print them onto the orange paper. Alternatively hand-write them with texta.

4. Cut each sign out so they're rectangular in shape, then cut out slightly larger rectangles from the white paper, which will provide a frame for the signs.

5. Glue the orange signs onto the white rectangles, then stick the signs onto the ends of the skewers with a piece of sticky tape across the back of each sign. Stick a sign into each jar.

6. Arrange the jars on the rustic wood and decorate around the jars with the black netting and spiders.

YOU WILL NEED:

- 4 glass jars
- Halloween-themed lollies (candies, sweets), including orange and black lollies, and body-part lollies, like lips and teeth
- sheet of orange paper
- black texta (marker pen; optional)
- scissors
- sheet of white paper
- craft glue
- 4 short skewers, about 10 cm (4 in) long
- sticky tape (Scotch tape)
- rustic piece of wood
- black netting
- plastic spiders

SKULL LIGHTS

When buying the skulls for this project, look for ones that have flat bases (rather than a hole) so that you can glue the base to the jar lid. Mind you, it isn't vital to glue the skulls down, although it will help keep your display in one piece.

WHAT TO DO

1. Glue a skull onto the lid of each jar. Allow to dry, so the skull is firmly stuck on.
2. Put a smaller skull (if using) and LED tea light (much safer than real ones) inside each jar. Put the lids on.
3. Drape some black netting or webbing over the skull, allowing it to hang down the sides of the jar.
4. Sit the jars on your mantelpiece, doorstep or wherever else you fancy and surround them with a few plastic spiders.
5. If you want to hang the jars up, you need to make a hanging loop around the top of them. To work out the length of twine or rope you'll need to make a hanging loop, wrap a piece of twine twice around the jar then make a loop roughly the length you want. Undo and measure the length you have used, adding on 5 cm (2 in) to make tying the knots easier. Make as many lengths as you need.
6. To make the hanging loop, take the measured twine and wrap it twice around the top of the jar (in the groove), tying it in a loose single knot once you've gone around twice. Next take the long end of the twine over the top of the jar to the opposite side and tuck it under both layers of twine – this is why the first knot needs to be loose, otherwise it's too hard to tuck the twine under. Pull the twine until you have the desired loop length and tie a tight knot. Re-tie the loose knot to make it tight too. Cut off any excess string. Note that if you aren't hanging the jars from hooks, you may want to leave tying the second knot until you have looped the twine over, for example, a tree branch.
7. Wait until it gets dark to turn the tea lights on, then get ready to be spooked!

YOU WILL NEED:

▼ craft glue

▼ plastic skulls (preferably with flat bases)

▼ empty jam or mason jars with lids

▼ extra smaller skulls for inside the jars (optional)

▼ LED tea lights

▼ black webbing or netting

▼ small plastic spiders

▼ black twine or rope (optional)

CHRISTMAS

Christmas is the time when you can really go to town and have lots of fun styling both inside and outside your home. Throughout this chapter you'll find ideas for simple and elegant styling projects, several of which are suitable to do with kids (and you'll be pleased to know, not one of them involves using an empty toilet roll!). None of the projects are particularly costly and many make use of things you may already have or that you can find in nature. At the end of the chapter, there are two themed Christmas projects, where you can go all out.

SIMPLE CHRISTMAS DECORATIONS

Although the shops are bursting with decorations to buy at Christmas, I still love to make one or two projects each year. I keep some from year to year, like the horizontal Christmas branch, while others I take apart after Christmas. Here is a selection of my favourites.

STAR DECORATIONS

While forming the twigs into the star shape for this project, I find it easier to keep them held together using elastic bands.

WHAT TO DO

1. To form the star shape, take two of the twigs and make a 'V' shape with them. Wrap an elastic band around the bottom of the V. Repeat with two more twigs.

2. Place the first V on a flat surface and invert it. Turn the second V almost 90 degrees and sit it on top of the first V, so that the bottom branch touches the tip of the other branch. Place the remaining twig in position to complete the star (use the photo below as a guide).

3. Wrap the remaining three elastic bands around the other three points of the star to hold everything in place.

4. Remove one elastic band. Take a length of wool about 20 cm (8 in) long and wrap it several times around the end of one star point, tying the two twigs together securely. Repeat with the other four points, ensuring all the knots are tied on the same side of the star. Snip off all the ends of the wool.

5. Take five additional 20 cm (8 in) lengths of wool and, one at a time, wrap these several times around the five inner points of the star where the twigs cross each other. Tie all the points securely, ensuring all the knots are on the same side as before, and snip off all the ends of the wool.

6. Decide how long you'd like the star to dangle, then double this length and cut a piece of wool to size. Fold the piece of wool in half to form a loop, and pass the loop under the top point of the star. Stick the other (loose) ends through the loop and pull gently to secure. Tie the two loose ends together so that the star is ready for hanging.

7. Hang as desired: these make great Christmas tree decorations, and also look pretty hanging in windows and on walls and doors.

YOU WILL NEED:

▼ 5 twigs of similar size, roughly 15 cm (6 in) in length

▼ 5 small elastic bands

▼ scissors

▼ red wool

SPEEDY WASHI-TAPE CHRISTMAS TREE CANVAS

These 'trees' are fun and festive, and are especially good if you don't have room for a big tree. They're also great for kids to make for decorating their bedrooms.

For added glamour and fun I put mine inside an empty frame. You can find old frames at second-hand shops and give them a quick coat of paint with white spray-paint. But you don't have to frame this canvas; you can simply hang it by itself or stand it on a shelf.

WHAT TO DO

1. Cut out lengths of washi tape in varying sizes to act as the 'branches' of the tree. The lengths will depend on how big your canvas is. The bottom branch should be about three-quarters of the width of the canvas. Each branch after that should be slightly smaller until you reach the apex of the tree. Again, the number of branches you'll need will depend on the width of the canvas – the example on this page uses 13 pieces, but yours might need more or less than that.

2. Using the photo as a guide, stick the pieces of washi tape onto the canvas, beginning at the bottom and working your way up.

3. Cut out another small piece of washi tape in a different colour to act as the tree trunk and add this to the canvas. You can also create little 'presents' with the washi tape, as in the photo.

4. Top the tree with a star made from washi tape, a cardboard star, a pompom or a 3D star. You could also add a few 3D ornaments with sticky tape if you like.

5. Stand your canvas up on a shelf or hang it on a wall using a picture hook. If using a frame, hang the frame on a wall with picture hooks, then hang the canvas tree inside the frame with another picture hook.

YOU WILL NEED

▼ scissors

▼ washi tape in colours/patterns of your choice

▼ stretched art canvas (the size will depend on how big you want the Christmas tree to be)

▼ cardboard star, pompom or 3D star (optional)

▼ 3D decorations (optional)

▼ sticky tape (Scotch tape; optional)

▼ picture hooks (optional)

▼ frame (optional)

- newspaper
- white spray-paint
- 1 long dead tree branch, with several smaller branches off the main branch
- battery-operated string of LED lights, with about 40–50 lights (available from party shops, Ikea, Christmas shops etc)
- sticky tape (Scotch tape; optional)
- 2 small eye-screw hooks or 2 drawing-pins (thumbtacks)
- tape measure or long ruler
- scissors
- ribbon or string to hang the branch (the length will depend on where you are hanging it from)
- Christmas decorations of your choice

HORIZONTAL CHRISTMAS BRANCH

This is one of my favourite decorations to put up at Christmas; I even have a special set of decorations that I keep from year to year just for this.

To find a tree branch, scour the ground of a local park, forest or some bushland. Never cut off a branch from a tree (unless the tree belongs to you). Look for one that has many side branches so you have several places to hang decorations from. These look great hanging over your Christmas table, over an island bench or in a high doorway.

Your branch can be as long as you want and will probably be determined by the space you want to hang it in and how many decorations you have. At 190 cm (75 in), mine is quite long, so choose a length that suits your room. If your branch and decorations are lightweight, you should be able to hang them with just drawing-pins. Alternatively, two small eye-screw hooks will work.

WHAT TO DO

1. Lay several sheets of newspaper outside or in a well-ventilated area and spray-paint the branch white. Allow to dry and then apply another coat if necessary. Leave to dry completely.

2   Wrap the string of lights around the branch, taping or tying the battery pack to the stump end of the branch, hiding it as much as possible.

3   Screw the two hooks into the ceiling or doorway where you want to hang the branch. The screws need to be positioned so the ribbon or string that's attached to the branch will hang about 10 cm (4 in) in from either end. If using drawing-pins, don't do this step yet.

4   Decide how low you'd like the branch to hang from the ceiling/doorway, measure this distance and then cut two pieces of ribbon or string just over twice that length.

5   It's helpful to have someone assist you with this step. Take one piece of ribbon and loop it around one end of the branch about 10 cm (4 in) in from the end. Tie both ends to the hook. Repeat with the other end of the branch. If using drawing-pins to hang your branch, loop the two pieces of ribbon around the branch at each end, then stick drawing-pins through the loose ends of the ribbon at the desired height.

6   Now the real fun begins! Hang your decorations from the branch; dangling them at different heights looks most effective.

HOMEMADE ADVENT CALENDAR

Instead of buying a traditional Advent calendar or one of the modern ones with chocolate in it, why not make your own? This way you can personalise it to suit your family. I'm not suggesting you fill the envelopes with 24 gifts, as that could become very expensive; it's more about writing messages to your children or suggesting things they can do.

The windows of traditional Advent calendars are replaced with paper-bag envelopes in this project. I generally pop a gift into a few of the envelopes (nothing expensive) and then write messages for the rest, but you can fill yours with whatever you wish. You can make one for each child in the family, or do as we do and take it in turns to open a number.

WHAT TO DO

1. Decorate the envelopes however you like using the washi tape. You could make a frame, a Christmas-tree outline or simply put strips of washi tape at the top and bottom of each bag – the options are endless!

2. Stamp the number 1 into the centre of the first bag, 2 onto the second, and so on, all the way to 24.

3. Using the silver or gold pen, write messages on either notepaper or cards (*see* opposite page for ideas) and put one message into each envelope. Also add any gifts you are using (spreading them out evenly over all the bags is a good idea) and fold over the top of each bag.

4. Secure each bag with either a clothes peg or paperclip.

5. Now you need to do a bit of planning. Arrange your bags how you want to hang them. I did mine in four rows of six bags and I hung them in number order, starting with 1 in the bottom left-hand corner. However, you can hang yours whichever way you like, and you may want to mix the numbers up. Arrange the bags on a table in the pattern you want, then turn them all over.

6. Cut the twine or ribbon into six equal pieces (if following my pattern), each 75 cm (30 in) long.

7. Tie the first length of twine to the bottom of the coathanger. Put the coathanger on the table above the bags then tape the twine securely to the backs of the first column of envelopes.

8. Repeat step 7 for the other five columns of envelopes until all 24 envelopes have been secured.

9. Hang the coathanger from a hook in the wall, adjusting the columns slightly if necessary.

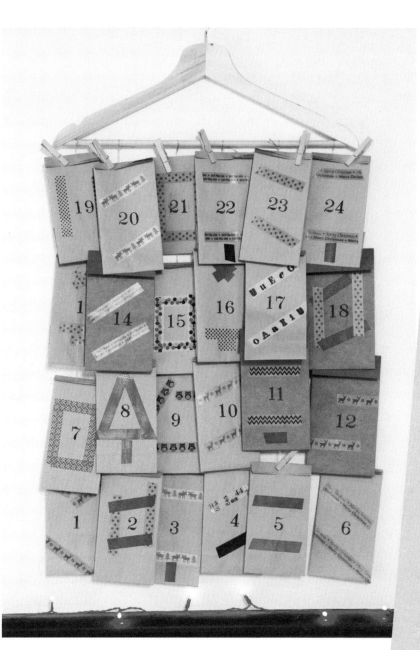

TREE-BRANCH SHINING STAR

Go to your local park, a forest or some bushland to look for fallen branches (don't cut branches from trees). If your own trees need pruning, trim them a few months in advance and store the branches so they get a lovely weathered look. I think the older and deader a branch is, the more beautiful it looks.

WHAT TO DO

YOU WILL NEED:

- ▼ 5 branches of similar size, roughly 90 cm (36 in) in length
- ▼ 5 elastic bands
- ▼ scissors
- ▼ strong rustic string or gardening twine
- ▼ string of outdoor LED lights, with about 40–50 lights, either solar-powered, plug-in or, if undercover, battery-operated (available from party shops, Ikea, Christmas shops etc)
- ▼ hook (optional)
- ▼ strong tape (optional)

1. Strip any leaves from the branches and remove any smaller branches. Carefully strip off the bark if you would like a more rustic look.

2. To form the star shape, take two of the branches and make a 'V' shape with them. Wrap an elastic band around the bottom of the V. Repeat with two more branches.

3. Place the first V on a flat surface and invert it. Turn the second V almost 90 degrees and sit it on top of the first V, so that the bottom branch touches the tip of the other branch. Place the remaining branch in position to complete the star (use the photo opposite as a guide).

4. Wrap the remaining three elastic bands around the other three points of the star to hold everything in place.

5. Remove one elastic band. Take a length of string about 50 cm (20 in) long and wrap it several times around the end of one star point, tying the two branches together securely. Repeat with the other four points, ensuring all the knots are tied on the same side of the star. Snip off all the ends of the string.

6. Take five additional 50 cm (20 in) lengths of string and, one at a time, wrap these several times around the five inner points of the star where the branches cross each other. Tie all the points securely, ensuring all the knots are on the same side as before, and snip off all the ends of the string.

7. Take the string of lights and, starting at one star point, wrap it around the five points of the star; try to keep the lights equally spaced.

8. Cut another piece of string about 60 cm (24 in) long (although this will depend on where you are hanging your star from and how low you want it to hang), fold it in half to form a loop, and pass the loop under the top point of the star. Stick the other (loose) ends through the loop and pull gently to secure. Tie the two loose ends together so that the star is ready for hanging.

9. Hang from a hook in the wall or in a window. If using plug-in lights, ensure your star is close to the power supply. If using battery-operated ones, you'll need to find somewhere to put the battery pack. It's best if it can be tucked out of sight; failing that, wrap any excess wire around the battery pack and secure it with strong tape to the wall.

BRANCH CHRISTMAS TREE CANVAS

The size and number of branches you will need for this project will depend on the size of your canvas. Ensure the branches aren't too thick or they'll be too heavy to stick to the canvas. You can leave your tree simple and plain without decorations (like the one pictured), or make it more playful and colourful by adding a few lightweight ornaments.

WHAT TO DO

1. Ensure the branches are clear of any protruding bits and strip off any bark, as this will prevent the branches from sticking to the canvas.

2. Lay the canvas down and create a Christmas-tree shape on it using the photo opposite as a guide. Apart from the tree 'trunk', the branches are placed horizontally and the LED lights will be added later to create the outline of the tree. Once you're happy with the shape, glue the branches to the canvas with a hot-glue gun or strong craft glue. For extra strength you can add a few (temporary) lengths of masking tape across each branch to help them stick securely to the canvas. Set aside until the glue has dried.

3. Once the branches are well stuck on, carefully remove the masking tape. Stand the tree up to ensure all the branches will stay securely in place.

4. Lay the tree down again. Use the string of lights to create the two sides and bottom of the tree, using the branches as support. If you find you are having trouble getting the lights to stay in place, secure them with strips of washi tape, making these a part of the design.

5. If using plug-in lights, ensure your canvas is close to the power supply. If using battery-operated ones, take any excess wire and the battery pack and tuck these behind the canvas out of sight (this is most neatly done at the top of the canvas). If you have excess lights they may well shine through the canvas, but this just adds to the look.

6. Glue the pompom or other lightweight ornament to the top of the tree to act as a star. You have now created the simplest version, so you can lean the canvas against a wall and leave it as is, or add a few more lightweight decorations, as desired, securing them with washi tape or double-sided tape.

YOU WILL NEED:

- about 15 small branches
- large stretched art canvas (the size will depend on how big you want the Christmas tree to be; the one pictured is 91 cm x 61 cm/36 in x 24 in)
- hot-glue gun or strong craft glue
- masking tape (optional)
- battery-operated string of LED lights, with about 20–30 lights (or plug-in lights if you don't intend to move the canvas; available from party shops, Ikea, Christmas shops etc)
- colourful washi tape (optional)
- large pompom or other lightweight ornament for a star
- lightweight decorations (optional)
- double-sided tape (optional)

TABLE DECORATIONS

Planning how I'm going to style my Christmas table starts long before Christmas, as I think up what colour scheme I would like or if I want a theme. Some of these decorations can sit on your table for the days or weeks leading up to Christmas, lending a Christmassy feel to your home for longer, while others are more suited just to Christmas Day.

TABLE CENTREPIECE

The method for this project described below is the simplest way to make this centrepiece. For even more pizzazz, you can also add lights to the branch. If you'd like to do this, you'll need a string of 20 to 30 LED lights, but this will depend on the size of your branch. Wrap the lights around the branch before putting the decorations on, ensuring some of the lights go right to the end of some of the branches.

If using battery-operated lights, it's best to use a vase with a wider neck so you can fill the vase with plastic baubles to hide the battery pack within the baubles. However, ensure the battery pack is accessible so you can turn the lights on and off. If you are placing this on a sideboard or shelf with a powerpoint nearby, use plug-in lights instead.

If you don't have a vase with a narrow neck you can still make this project. To use a wider-necked vase, you will need to buy about 30 small silver plastic baubles (the actual number will depend on how big your vase is). The best place to buy these is at discount shops; they need to be plastic so they don't break. Press a ball of Blu Tack into the base of the vase, but don't squash it flat. Stick the base of the branch into the Blu Tack, then add the plastic baubles to the vase, pressing them in gently so they hold the branch in place. Then your branch is ready to decorate.

WHAT TO DO

1. Lay several sheets of newspaper outside or in a well-ventilated area and spray-paint the branch white. Allow to dry and then apply another coat if necessary. Leave to dry completely.

2. Put the branch into the vase. If it's a little wobbly, put a ball of Blu Tack in the bottom of the vase and stick the branch into that. Try to ensure you can't see the Blu Tack.

3. Adorn the branch with your choice of decorations, ensuring you don't hang heavy ornaments on fragile smaller branches.

UPSIDE-DOWN WREATH

This wreath, which hangs upside-down from the ceiling, provides a lovely alternative to a conventional bunch of flowers on your Christmas table.

WHAT TO DO

1 Using the secateurs, trim the stems of the foliage so everything is of similar length.

2 Tie the foliage together with rustic string, wrapping the string around the base of the foliage bunch several times. Secure the bunch by tying a knot.

3 Measure the distance from your ceiling to how low you want the bottom of the wreath to hang (the bottom being the tied-together ends). Cut a length of string twice this measurement, adding on an extra 20 cm (8 in) or so, then also wrap this around the base of the foliage bunch and tie in a knot, leaving two long ends (this is what you'll use to hang the wreath from the ceiling). Tie these two ends together to form a loop.

4 This step is optional, but it adds additional decoration and makes the wreath look neater. Wrap the ribbon around the string on the foliage and tie it in a neat bow. To get a bow that looks elegant and sits flat, tie the knot as normal and form the first loop. For the second loop, go behind the first loop instead of in front (which is more usual) and then form the second loop. Gently tighten the bow.

5 Working with the wreath flat on a table, tie the silver or glass ornaments onto the foliage stems with silver twine, ensuring they are securely tied on so they don't fall off and break (if glass) once you've hung the wreath. Ensure the ornaments are evenly placed around the wreath.

6 Put an eye-screw hook into the ceiling and hang the wreath over your dining table. You can always rearrange the ornaments once the wreath is hanging if you aren't happy with their positions; just be careful not to drop them.

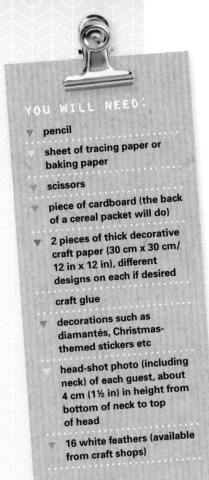

ANGEL PLACE SETTINGS

These are probably my favourite place settings. I kept the first version I made of these for many years and brought them out every Christmas for a while – I loved looking back at the photos of my kids and seeing how they'd grown.

These can be as stylish or as fun as you like. They're great for kids to help make too; you could even use plain white cardboard and ask the kids to decorate the card before you make the angels.

Makes 8 place settings

WHAT TO DO

1. Using the pencil and tracing paper or baking paper, trace around the angel template on p. 180 and cut it out.

2. Trace around this cut-out onto the cardboard and cut this out to form your own template.

3. Trace this template eight times onto the two pieces of craft paper (i.e. four on each sheet) and carefully cut the angel shapes out.

4. To make slits for the wings, cut a 1 cm (½ in) slit about 2.5 cm (1 in) down from the top curve and 1.5 cm (½ in) in from one of the edges. Repeat on the other side of the angel body, then repeat for the seven remaining angels.

5. Working on one angel at a time, put craft glue onto one of the straight edges, then curl this around to form the body, sticking it to the other straight edge. Make sure you don't cover the wing slits. Press the edges firmly together to seal. Leave to dry.

6. Decorate the angel bodies with diamantés, Christmas-themed stickers and/or any other embellishments you'd like.

7. Cut out the heads from your photos, including the neck. Put some glue onto the necks (on the photo side of the paper) and stick these onto the insides of the angel bodies.

8. Poke a feather into each slit on each angel (i.e. two feathers per angel) to create the wings and arrange your choir of angels on the Christmas table.

PINE CONE PLACE SETTINGS

To make these you need to find pine cones that have opened. However, if you're looking for pine cones on the forest floor and you can only find ones that haven't opened up yet, take these home and they should open within a week or so. Paint the top third tips of each pine cone in your colour of choice (green works well) and leave to dry. Write or stamp name tags for each guest on a small piece of card and sit these on the top of each pine cone to denote place settings.

OLD PEG PLACE SETTINGS

To make these, you'll need to buy some old clothes pegs (or find new 'old' ones). Write your guests' names on luggage tags then thread rustic or coloured twine through the luggage tag holes. Tie each tag to a peg, about a third of the way from the top of the peg, then sit these on top of napkins at each guest's allocated spot.

SCRABBLE LETTER PLACE SETTINGS

These are super simple yet very effective. Arrange guests' names on top of a napkin on their plate using scrabble letters. You can often find old scrabble letters in second-hand shops, or use them from your own set. You can also buy magnetic scrabble letters in some gift shops. Any will work well. If you don't have sufficient letters for whole names, just use first and last initials.

Not only am I obsessed with luggage tags, I'm also obsessed with reindeer and stag heads – of the paper or cardboard variety, of course! The silhouette of a stag head is instantly recognisable and doesn't have to be restricted to Christmas; however, in this theme we are going all Christmassy. Complete your table with a white tablecloth.

You can photocopy the stag head template that's included on p. 181 and use it for the Reindeer Toppers and Table Decorations projects.

CANDLE CENTREPIECE

This is a simple centrepiece that you can make as big or as small as you like.

WHAT TO DO

1. Bend the Christmas tree branches into a circle that is about 20 cm (8 in) in diameter. Tie the branches together with the florist's wire.

2. Wrap each piece of the red-and-white twine several times around the bottom third of each candle, securing with a knot.

3. Place the foliage circle on a plate of a similar size and put the candles inside the circle.

4. Stick the reindeer toppers into the foliage, hiding the toothpicks in the greenery.

YOU WILL NEED:

▼ 2–3 long fresh Christmas tree branches or other bushy greenery

▼ florist's wire

▼ 3 lengths of red-and-white striped twine, each about 90 cm (36 in) long

▼ 3 white pillar candles (I used ones that are about 14 cm/ 5½ in high and 6.5 cm/ 2½ in across the bottom)

▼ plate with a diameter of about 25 cm (10 in)

▼ 5 reindeer 'toppers' (*see* p. 165)

REINDEER TABLE DECORATIONS

Continue the gorgeous reindeer theme with these reindeer table decorations. You could also make them into place settings by printing out your guests' names using an old-fashioned Dymo label maker (or just printer labels) and sticking a name onto each reindeer.

Makes 8 reindeers

WHAT TO DO

1. Cut out the stag head template and draw around it onto the back of the sheets of silver cardboard. Do this eight times, making sure the stag heads don't overlap. Keep the drawings quite close together as you will need the leftover cardboard. Carefully cut out the stag heads.

2. Cut the ribbon into eight equal pieces, each 25 cm (10 in) long. Tie the ribbon in a bow around the base of one of the antlers on each stag head. To get a bow that looks elegant and sits flat, tie the knot as normal and form the first loop. For the second loop, go behind the first loop instead of in front (which is more usual) and then form the second loop. Gently tighten the bow.

3. If you are planning to add names to the reindeer heads so you can use them as place settings, do this now.

4. Next you need to make the supports that hold the reindeers up. Using the leftover cardboard, cut out eight strips about 12 cm x 1 cm (5 in x ½ in) in size. Fold 4 cm (1½ in) of the cardboard over and glue this (on the plain side) to the back of the stag head at the base (so that the longer length is sticking out and acting as the support). Make sure these strips are centred down the middle of the reindeer noses when you glue them on, otherwise the reindeers may topple over.

5. Arrange the reindeers around the table, placing one close to each guest's setting (especially if using them as place settings!).

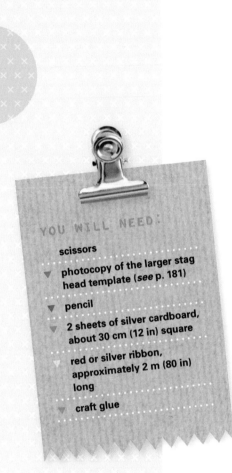

YOU WILL NEED:

- scissors
- photocopy of the larger stag head template (*see* p. 181)
- pencil
- 2 sheets of silver cardboard, about 30 cm (12 in) square
- red or silver ribbon, approximately 2 m (80 in) long
- craft glue

REINDEER TOPPERS

These are very cute and add an instant sense of Christmas to your table! Although this isn't specifically aimed at kids, I'm sure most kids would love to make these, but they may need a bit of help cutting around the antlers. I use these in the candle centrepiece (*see* p. 163), but you can also stick them into the top of canapés or other Christmas food.

Makes 5 toppers

WHAT TO DO

1. Cut out the stag head template and draw around it onto the back of the piece of silver cardboard. Do this five times, making sure the stag heads don't overlap. Cut out the five stag heads. At this point, I like to colour the back of each stag head with the silver pen so it looks good from all angles, but this is up to you.

2. Using sticky tape, stick one end of a toothpick onto the back of each stag head, ensuring the toothpick doesn't stick out the top.

3. Stick a red jewel or sticker onto each reindeer's nose.

4. Stick the toppers into the greenery of your candle centrepiece (*see* p. 163) at even intervals, or use them to decorate canapés or other Christmas food.

YOU WILL NEED:

- scissors
- photocopy of the smaller stag head template (*see* p. 181)
- pencil
- sparkly silver cardboard (or your choice of colour)
- silver pen (optional)
- sticky tape (Scotch tape)
- 5 toothpicks
- 5 red jewels or stickers (for the noses)

CINNAMON-STICK NAPKINS

These look best with long cinnamon sticks, which you can find in delis and spice shops. Shorter ones will work fine as well, though, if you can't find the longer ones.

Makes 8 napkins

YOU WILL NEED:

▼ iron and ironing board

▼ 8 white napkins

▼ thin silver ribbon or silver twine

▼ 8 long cinnamon sticks

▼ 8 small pieces of Christmas tree or other greenery

WHAT TO DO

1. Iron and fold the napkins, and put a napkin in the centre of each place setting.

2. Using the ribbon or twine, tie a cinnamon stick and a piece of greenery together a couple of centimetres from the bottom, leaving the ribbon ends loose (or you could tie these in a bow, if desired).

3. Place one decoration on top of each napkin.

STYLING YOUR CHRISTMAS TABLE

Here are a few hints and tips when stlying your table.

▼ Scatter the table with coloured stars (available from craft shops) in a colour to match your theme.

▼ If adding a table centrepiece keep it low so guests can still talk across the table to each other. If your centrepiece is tall, keep it narrow. If you really want to have a larger centrepiece, I would recommend moving it off the table once the meal is served.

▼ If using tea lights on the table I recommend using battery operated LED ones for safety.

NATURE AND LINEN THEME

This theme works just as well for a Northern Hemisphere snowy Christmas as a boiling-hot Down Under one. Complete the look with a linen tablecloth; if you don't have one, buy a piece of linen or linen-type fabric and fray the edges to match the napkins (see p. 170).

WEATHERED WOOD AND FOLIAGE TABLE WREATH

The size of the wreath will depend on how many twigs you have. Feel free to use more than what's suggested here.

WHAT TO DO

1. Before you stick all the pieces of wood together permanently, have a practice run, stacking them on top of each other in circular layers. You'll need about five layers altogether. This will help you determine the size of the final wreath, especially if you are using more than 30 pieces of wood.

2. Remove three layers of wood so you're left with just the first two layers.

3. Working slowly and carefully, start by gluing the first two layers together at points where the wood touches.

4. Attach another layer of wood and repeat step 3, then repeat with the next two layers (so you'll end up with five layers of wood, although the distinct layers can be quite hard to see).

5. Sit the wreath on the piece of cardboard and draw around it roughly with the pencil. Remove the wreath and draw another circle inside the roughly drawn one about 2 cm (¾ in) in from the edge. Cut out the smaller circle and set aside.

6. Thread the rosemary into the wreath, tucking it under one or two pieces of wood to keep it in place (you shouldn't need to attach it with anything).

7. Put the cardboard circle where you are going to place your wreath, sit the wreath on top of the cardboard and then place the candle(s) in the middle. Never leave lit candles unattended.

HOMEMADE LINEN 'YUM' NAPKINS

Linen napkins are a beautiful choice for your table, but they can be pretty expensive to buy. The good news is they are easy to make yourself. These napkins are about 48 cm x 38 cm (19 in x 15 in) in size, but you can make them bigger or smaller if you prefer. Their frayed edges are visually appealing, and also mean there's no hemming involved!

You could also make a matching table runner 30–40 cm (12–16 in) wide and the length of your table, plus an extra 30 cm (12 in) for overhang.

Makes 8 napkins

WHAT TO DO

1. Using the ruler and chalk, draw 8 rectangles onto the piece of linen, each one measuring 48 cm x 38 cm (19 in x 15 in).

2. Carefully cut out each napkin.

3. Working on one napkin at a time, find a loose thread on an edge and start pulling it. Keep pulling it around all sides of the napkin several times until you have a frayed edge of about 1 cm (½ in) all the way around.

4. Iron the napkins, then fold them in half (along the longest sides), then into thirds to make a rectangle approximately 24 cm x 12 cm (9½ in x 5 in).

5. Using the red fabric paint and the paintbrush, paint the word 'YUM' onto the bottom of each napkin (i.e. on the short side of the folded napkins).

6. Set aside for several hours until completely dry, then place a napkin on top of a dinner plate at each place setting. Finish by putting a leaf decoration (*see* p. 171) on top of each folded napkin, above the word 'YUM'.

YOU WILL NEED:

- ruler
- piece of chalk
- piece of linen sufficient to make 8 napkins, each 48 cm x 38 cm (19 in x 15 in) in size (the length the linen needs to be will depend on its width)
- scissors
- iron and ironing board
- red fabric paint
- paintbrush

CHRISTMAS BAUBLE DECORATIONS

A very simple but effective table decoration is to arrange a small selection of beautiful baubles on a cake stand. You could also add a silver spray-painted leaf (*see* opposite page) if you like.

LEAF DECORATIONS

If you are using fresh leaves, as opposed to crisp autumn or winter ones, start this project one week before you need the decorations, as it takes that long for fresh leaves to be nicely flattened.

Makes 8 leaf decorations

WHAT TO DO

1. If using fresh leaves, put each leaf between two sheets of paper towel and then place these between the pages of a heavy book. Leave for one week to flatten and dry out slightly. (There is no need to do this if your leaves are already dry.) After the week is up, remove the leaves from the book.

2. Lay down a few sheets of newspaper and spray-paint the leaves with either silver or gold paint; make sure you do this outside or in a well-ventilated space. Leave to dry completely.

3. Once the leaves are dry, put one at each person's place setting, sitting it on their napkin. If you made a few extra, scatter these elsewhere on the table.

YOU WILL NEED

▼ 8 large undamaged leaves (it's a good idea to find a few extra in case of mistakes)

▼ 16 sheets of paper towel (if using fresh leaves)

▼ heavy book (if using fresh leaves)

▼ newspaper

▼ silver or gold spray-paint

HANDY HINTS, MATERIALS AND RECIPES

The following section contains helpful 'how to' instructions that are used in a number of projects in this book and can be applied to your own adventures into styling. It also provides some background info on materials/equipment you may not be overly familiar with (e.g. Dymo label makers) and recipes for basic cupcakes and biscuits that you can decorate.

HOW TO HANG JARS WITH STRING

It's important to get these hanging loops right otherwise the jars you've spent time decorating could drop and smash.

1. To work out the length of string you'll need to make a hanging loop, wrap a piece of string twice around the jar then make a loop roughly the length you want. Undo and measure the length you have used, adding on 5 cm (2 in) to make tying the knots easier.

2. Take the measured string and wrap it twice around the top of the jar (in the groove), tying it in a loose single knot once you've gone around twice. Next take the long end of the string over the top of the jar to the opposite side and tuck it under both layers of string – this is why the first knot needs to be loose, otherwise it's too hard to tuck the string under. Pull the string until you have the desired loop length and tie a tight knot. Re-tie the loose knot to make it tight too. Cut off any excess string. Note that if you aren't hanging the jars from hooks, you may want to leave tying the second knot until you have looped the string over the tree branch or wherever you are hanging it from.

HOW TO TIE THE PERFECT BOW

To tie a bow that looks elegant and sits flat, tie the knot as normal and form the first loop. For the second loop, go behind the first loop instead of in front (which is more usual) and then form the second loop. Gently tighten the bow.

HOW TO THREAD TWINE
THROUGH LUGGAGE TAGS

Following are a few suggestions of how to thread twine through luggage tag holes, after which you can attach the tags to whatever you like.

▼ Loop: Double the piece of twine over and thread about 2 cm (¾ in) of the folded end through the tag hole. Thread the loose ends of the twine through the loop created by the folded end and pull gently to secure.

▼ Simple knot: Thread the twine through the hole until it is halfway along the twine's length, then tie a knot next to the hole, leaving the ends loose.

▼ Simple bow: Allowing extra twine for the bow, tie a simple knot at the hole (as in number 2 above) then carefully tie a bow with the loose ends (*see* How to Tie the Perfect Bow, opposite page).

▼ Simple hang: The easiest of the lot! Simply thread the twine through the tag hole then tie or tape the tag directly onto your gift, Christmas tree branch etc.

HOW TO FIGURE OUT
HOW MUCH TWINE TO USE

How much twine you need for luggage tags – and whether you need twine or not – will depend on what you are using the luggage tags for. If tying them around jars, you will need to measure around each jar and add about 10 cm (4 in) before cutting each piece. If using your tags as place settings that will be tied around napkins, decide how many times you want the twine to go around each napkin (several loops are often more effective than just one), then cut each piece of twine to this length.

A luggage tag for a gift needs about 25–30 cm (10–12 in) of twine – you can either tie the tag to the ribbon, if using, or simply attach the tag to the present by sticking a short length of washi tape or sticky tape across the twine. If using tags to label boxes, you probably won't need any twine at all as you'll simply stick the tag onto the box.

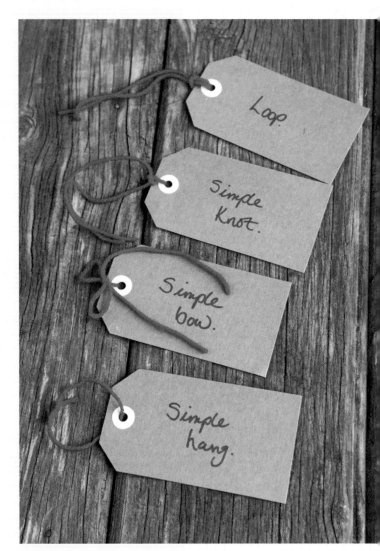

HOW TO MAKE A POTATO STAMP

You were probably a kid the last time you made a potato stamp, but they are very simple to make and far less time consuming than trying to find the exact rubber stamp you need for a project.

People's initials are the easiest stamps to make, and the larger the image, the easier it is to carve.

1 To make a potato stamp, either draw or print off the image you want to stamp. Ensure the image is the correct size for your project.

2 Slice a potato in half top to bottom and place your image back-to-front on the potato (so it's the right way around when you stamp it). Draw around the image with a pen or sharp pencil, including any inside detail, such as the triangle on an 'A'.

3 Using a sharp knife carefully cut around the shape, slicing away the potato, so that all you are left with is the shape of your image. Cut out about 1 cm (½ in) from any inside detail. Put the potato upside down on paper towel to absorb any excess moisture.

4 Put some craft or fabric paint on a plate or tray and brush the image all over with a thin layer of paint. Do a practise run on a piece of paper to ensure the design stamps properly; you may need to shave off a few ragged edges.

5 Once you are happy with how the potato is stamping, put some more paint onto the stamp and you're ready to go. Reapply paint each time you stamp.

HOW TO WRAP A PRESENT AND TIE WITH STRING

In my opinion, how a present is wrapped and presented is important – it's not just about the gift, it's about how I wrap it too.

1 It might sound obvious, but cut the wrapping paper to the size you need rather than having huge amounts of excess paper wrapped around or folded over at the ends.

2 When wrapping the ends, ensure you have sharp neat folds and try to use just one piece of tape for each join.

3 Tying with string or twine adds another dimension to your wrapping. Think about the design before tying it, although it's not that hard to undo it if you decide you don't like it. A simple cross shape is the easiest to do, but you can also go crazy and tie twine around and around many times both horizontally and vertically. Unless the knot or bow is part of the design, keep it at the back of the present.

WHAT IS WASHI TAPE?

Washi tape is basically patterned masking tape and comes in literally thousands of different designs. It can be used on a multitude of projects both for practical and design reasons. I keep a selection of different patterned tapes to hand to quickly make a gift tag or for wrapping gifts. It is useful for wrapping presents, not only because it can add fun to your parcel, but also because it isn't quite as sticky as sticky tape so it can be easily removed if you make a mistake. You can buy it at craft shops, haberdasheries and some office supply stores.

WHAT IS A DYMO?

Dymos are label makers. You can buy modern ones from office supply shops, but the old-fashioned ones have a much more recognisable (and fun) font. Whenever I see old-fashioned Dymo lettering, I'm instantly transported back to my childhood when they were the 'in' thing to have. They are useful for adding an instant retro feel to a project, and it's often a lot easier and quicker to print out a Dymo message than it is to find and print a particular font from your computer.

WHAT ARE TYPOGRAPHY SETS?

Typography sets are individual letter and/or number stamps that you can use with an ink pad to create messages. They can be found in many craft shops and some gift shops. Some stamps are designed so you can stamp a whole word at a time (rather than letter by letter), but more often than not you have to stamp the letters one by one.

I bought my first typography set partly because I loved the box it came in, and also because I was inspired by the thought of all the things I could do with the stamps, even though I didn't have a specific project in mind at the time. I have since used it for endless projects, many of which are in this book.

A few things to keep in mind when using typography sets:

▼ Always practise stamping before doing the final run. Practise on scrap paper to make sure the words or message you want to use will fit into the space you've got or to work out your design.

▼ Replenish the ink after each stamping, unless you are going for a particular look where you don't want much ink on each letter.

▼ If changing colours, ensure you clean all the previous ink off before stamping the next colour.

▼ Stamp each letter firmly and evenly, but don't press to the sides or you may end up with the edges of the stamp inked on too.

BISCUIT RECIPE

Makes about 16 biscuits

1. Put the butter and sugar in a large bowl and beat together using electric beaters, until light and fluffy.
2. Beat in the egg, then stir in the flour.
3. Using your hands bring the mixture together into a ball. Wrap in plastic wrap and chill in the fridge for about 30 minutes.
4. Preheat oven to 175°C (350°F). Roll out the dough on a floured work surface or sheet of baking paper to about 5 mm (¼ in) thickness.
5. Using cookie cutters of your choice (e.g. love hearts, racing cars etc), cut out shapes from the biscuit dough. If you like, make some of them so they can hang from a ribbon and be used as decorations. To do this, use a skewer to poke a hole in the top of some of the shapes.
6. Put the biscuits on baking paper–lined trays and bake for about 15 minutes until light golden. For any biscuits that have a hole, gently poke the hole again after they're baked to ensure the hole is still there when they cool.
7. Cool on wire racks, then decorate. Thread ribbon through any biscuits with a hole.

YOU WILL NEED:

- 75 g (2¾ oz) butter, softened
- 150 g (5¼ oz) caster (superfine) sugar
- 1 egg, lightly beaten
- 175 g (6 oz) plain (all-purpose) flour
- thin ribbon, in the colour of your choice (optional)

CHOCOLATE CUPCAKES RECIPE

Makes 12 cupcakes

1. Preheat oven to 180°C (350°F) and line a 12-hole (capacity 80 ml or ⅓ cup) muffin tin with patty pans.
2. Put the butter, sugar and vanilla essence into a bowl and beat with an electric mixer, until pale and soft.
3. In a separate bowl sift the flour and cocoa powder together.
4. Add the eggs to the butter mixture one at a time, and beat until just combined.
5. Next add the milk and flour/cocoa alternately in small amounts and stir with a wooden spoon until just combined. Do not over-mix.
6. Divide the mixture evenly between the patty pans, then bake for 15–20 minutes or until cooked through.
7. Remove from the oven, leave in the tin for 5 minutes then transfer to a wire rack to cool completely. Store in an airtight container.

YOU WILL NEED:

- 100 g (3½ oz) butter, softened
- 185 g (6½ oz) caster (superfine) sugar
- ½ teaspoon vanilla essence
- 180 g (6½ oz) self-raising flour
- 2 tablespoons cocoa powder
- 2 eggs
- 125 ml (½ cup) milk

ANGEL
TEMPLATE

STAG HEAD
TEMPLATE

ABOUT THE AUTHOR

Katy Holder has had a long and successful career as a food stylist and writer. In this book she embraces general table and home styling, something she has always loved. Katy grew up in London, but Sydney has been her home now for many years. While living in Tokyo for a few years, she fell in love with Japanese style and styling, and the beautiful ceramics the Japanese create. Katy's aim for this book is to show you how to create simple but effective styling ideas for both your home and garden. Katy is also the author of *Hungry Campers Cookbook* and *A Moveable Feast*, and currently writes the food pages for Australia's *marie claire* magazine.

AUTHOR
ACKNOWLEDGEMENTS

Putting this book together was great fun, but it was also a huge undertaking and there are many people I would like to thank for helping me bring *Styling Made Simple* to life. The biggest thank you must go, once again, to my photographer, Natasha Milne. As with my previous two books, Tash went above and beyond a normal day's work to help me create a book packed full of great photos that illustrate every single project. Tash, you are brilliant.

A massive thank you also to my editor, Michelle Bennett, who tirelessly questioned every project, urging me to add more detail for the non-creative types among us. Michelle was sufficiently inspired by the book to make some of the projects during the book's creation! Thank you.

At my publisher, Hardie Grant, I would like to thank Melissa Kayser for encouraging me to write this book, and Marg Bowman, who took up the reins part way through the project.

I must also thank my gorgeous little models Lily, Abby, Zac, Mason, Max and Jack. I had so much fun creating those parties.

And last but not least to my friends who worked both day and night during the shoot to help me create the projects ready for being photographed. Thank you Sarah and Karen – I am truly grateful. And thank you to my family – to Alex for making the beautiful Christmas weathered wood wreath and to Max and Jack for your endless foraging for branches and twigs.

I would like to say a very big thank you to Spotlight for providing the materials needed to make many of the projects in this book.
Go to **www.spotlight.com.au** to find your nearest store.

Thanks also to Mud Australia for supplying props for the photo shoot.

ACKNOWLEDGEMENTS

The publisher would like to acknowledge the following individuals and organisations:

Editorial manager
Marg Bowman

Project manager
Marg Bowman

Editor
Michelle Bennett

Design
Erika Budiman

Typesetting
Megan Ellis

Photography
Natasha Milne

Pre-press
Megan Ellis, Splitting Image

Additional images appearing throughout the book:
Cover background: Blue Wooden Wall, Imageman/shutterstock.com
Polaroid surrounds: Andrey_Kuzmin/shutterstock.com

Explore Australia Publishing Pty Ltd
Ground Floor, Building 1, 658 Church Street,
Richmond, VIC 3121

Explore Australia Publishing Pty Ltd is a division of Hardie Grant Publishing Pty Ltd

hardie grant publishing

Published by Explore Australia Publishing Pty Ltd, 2015

Form and design © Explore Australia Publishing Pty Ltd, 2015
Concept and text © Katy Holder, 2015

A Cataloguing-in-Publication entry is available from the catalogue of the National Library of Australia at www.nla.gov.au

ISBN-13 9781741174915

10 9 8 7 6 5 4 3 2 1

Printed and bound in China by Leo Paper Products Ltd

Publisher's note: Every effort has been made to ensure that the information in this book is accurate at the time of going to press. The publisher welcomes information and suggestions for correction or improvement. Email: info@exploreaustralia.net.au

www.exploreaustralia.net.au
Follow us on Twitter: @ExploreAus
Find us on Facebook: www.facebook.com/exploreaustralia